Night (1907)
William Orpen (1878–1931)

FORGOTTEN BEAUTY

IRISH LOVE POETRY ACROSS THE CENTURIES

WITH PAINTINGS BY CELEBRATED IRISH ARTISTS

SELECTED AND INTRODUCED BY BRIAN LALOR

Gill & Macmillan

For a long-anticipated Wicklow wain

Published in Ireland by
Gill & Macmillan
Hume Avenue, Park West, Dublin 12
www.gillmacmillanbooks.ie

Introduction © Brian Lalor 2014
ISBN 978 0 7171 5779 2

Concept and design © Bookcraft Ltd 2014   www.bookcraft.co.uk
Project managed by John Button
Designed by Lucy Guenot
Editorial and rights management by Julie Laws

Set in 12 on 19 point Plantin.

A CIP catalogue record for this book is available from the British Library.

Printed by Imago

CONTENTS

INTRODUCTION

BRIAN LALOR

The language of love poetry is not only universal, but also timeless. It has existed in some form throughout the centuries, as men and women have sought to express their affection for each other. Love lyrics from the earliest recorded writings do not differ in feeling from lines written by poets in more recent centuries. However, the earliest known love poems frequently lack sophistication of language. A plausible explanation is that the difficulties of translating dead languages make refinements of expression more elusive. In one of the earliest known love lyrics, from *c.*2000 BC, inscribed on a clay tablet in the Sumerian city of Nippur, a woman speaks passionately to her lover:

> Bridegroom, dear to my heart,
> Goodly is your beauty,
> Honeysweet.
> You have captivated me,
> Let me stand trembling before you:
> Bridegroom, I would be taken to the bedchamber.
>
> Anon, 'Bridegroom, Dear to my Heart', Sumerian

Later, from the New Kingdom in Egypt, *c.*1500 BC, we hear another woman's voice, thinking of her lover. The form here is doggerel:

> I hear thy voice, O turtle dove,
> The dawn is still aglow –
> For I have found my dear, my love,
> And I am by his side.
> I am the fairest in the land
> For he has called me so.
>
> Anon, 'I Hear thy Voice, O Turtle Dove', Egyptian

These lines, simple and ingenuous, could be from a present-day pop-music lyric, a suitable candidate for the Eurovision Song Contest. Later, from the eighth century BC, we hear the voice of a man. The verse is from the Hebrew Old Testament, and the lines are attributed, however unreliably, to a named individual, King Solomon. The language is more skilful, yet the image of the dove strikes a common chord and represents a theme of nature imagery often encountered in love poetry, the lover identifying with the tranquillity and beauty to be experienced in pastoral surroundings. Such nature imagery is particularly significant in defining much of the character of Irish love poetry:

> Behold, thou art fair, my love; behold
> thou art fair; thou hast doves' eyes
> Behold thou art fair, my love; my beloved,
> yea, pleasant: also, our bed is green.
>
> The Song of Solomon, I: 15–16, King James translation

Irish love poetry is of great lyrical and emotional richness and distinction, both in reflecting Irish sensibilities from the earliest writings to the present, and in belonging to a worldwide language of human emotional attachments. Allied to a strong reliance on nature imagery is the phenomenon of writing in two contemporaneous languages, Irish and English, with each language deriving influences from and increasing the range of the other.

The earliest poetry in Ireland was carried from the oral tradition of the Bronze and Iron Age inhabitants of the island into the written word, and transmitted to later generations by the recording of Christian monastic scribes. It is from the manuscripts of the monasteries that the voice of the poet in Irish society is first heard, as marginal glosses on ecclesiastical manuscripts, and in the compiling of the legends and mythology of pre-Christian society.

Throughout time, following invasions or through cultural exchanges acquired by study abroad, or through the influx of scholars and literary styles from elsewhere, the poetic manners of succeeding centuries became merged with the native traditions. Irish poetry has always followed its own path, but has also continually reflected influences from Britain, Continental Europe and the wider cultural world. Thus we have the terse and candid lyrics of the ninth to twelfth centuries AD in Old and Middle Irish; the formal romances of *amour courtois* in Latin, French, English or Irish in the thirteenth to sixteenth centuries; Classicism in English and the more rustic Gaelic court poetry in Irish during the seventeenth and eighteenth centuries; Romanticism, Symbolism and the Celtic Twilight in the nineteenth century; and, finally, Modernism in the present.

In this anthology of Irish love poetry, some of the most celebrated Irish writers will be found in conjunction with anonymous poets whose names, like those of the Sumerian and Egyptian writers, were probably known to their contemporaries, but are now lost to the written record.

Amongst the compositions of these anonymous authors are extraordinarily powerful and evocative poems, worthy of the greatest of Irish writers. In 'Dónal Óg', an Irish-language poem from the early nineteenth century, we find lines that are as superb nature writing as they are love poetry. In a commonly expressed theme, the voice is that of a woman whose trust in her lover has been betrayed:

> It is late last night the dog was speaking of you;
> the snipe was speaking of you in her deep marsh.
> It is you are the lonely bird through the woods;
> and that you may be without a mate until you find me.
>
> You have taken the east from me; you have taken the west from me;
> you have taken what is before me and what is behind me;
> you have taken the moon, you have taken the sun from me;
> and my fear is great that you have taken God from me!

> Anon, 'Dónal Óg', translated by Lady Gregory

Jonathan Swift and W.B. Yeats are undoubtedly the Irish writers most closely associated with long-term amorous relationships that informed their poetry: Swift in his love for Esther Johnson, whom he called Stella (although the actual nature of their relationship, certainly an intellectual one, is surrounded by ambiguity); and Yeats in his unrequited passion for the fiery and politically active Maud Gonne (though even as Yeats was addressing poems to her, Gonne was spurning his ardent pursuit and flood of love poems in favour of other lovers). The measured language of Swift, with its subdued and well-mannered emotion, can be contrasted with the more high-octane declarations of Yeats. Swift's affectionate birthday poem to Stella is prophetic, since she was to die the following year.

> This Day then, let us not be told,
> That you are sick, and I grown old
> Nor think on our approaching ills,
> And talk of Spectacles and Pills;

> Jonathan Swift, 'Stella's Birth-Day'

Winter, 1911
Harriet Hockley Townshend (1877–1941)

Reverie, 1882
Frank O'Meara (1853–1888)

Why should I blame her that she fill my days
With misery, or that she would of late
Have taught to ignorant men most violent ways,
Or hurled the little streets upon the great,

W.B. Yeats, 'No Second Troy'

Patrick Kavanagh, in his poetry, is more a lover of nature than of women, yet he has contributed a single poem to the vernacular tradition, a poem that has become one of the most popular and widely sung of Irish contemporary folk songs. In this case his authorship is not in doubt. Like Yeats before him, frustrated in love, he produced bitterly beautiful lines to an existing tune, 'The Dawning of the Day':

On Grafton Street in November we tripped lightly along
    the ledge
Of the deep ravine where can be seen the worth of
    passion's pledge,
The Queen of Hearts still making tarts and I not
    making hay –
O I loved too much and by such by such is happiness
    thrown away.

Patrick Kavanagh, 'On Raglan Road'

The vernacular tradition is the area where the world of the anonymous lyric merges with that of the work of acknowledged writers, and the compositions of known authors pass into the public domain as elements of the popular repertoire. Other poets who have had their poems adopted by the popular tradition (and often understood to be such) include Thomas Moore and Gerald Griffin. For a poem to merge into vernacular culture is an accolade to any writer. Oliver Goldsmith, when a student at Trinity College, used to slip out at night from his studies to hear his lyrics sung in the ale-houses of the city.

The poems included in this anthology are gathered under a number of themes that represent some of the many aspects of the love poem. There could be many more subdivisions, so myriad are the subtleties of love poetry, and so delicately nuanced is this area of expression. Individual lines and phrases can encapsulate a mood, an emotion, and a state of mind or a memory, with such precision that the feelings of the lover come vividly to life.

Sir John Sheepshanks and His Maid (1832–34)
William Mulready (1786–1863)

Despite the inclusion of two quotations from women of antiquity, the woman's voice is the most difficult to detect in a body of writing that has, from the earliest poems, been dominated by the male voice. Nonetheless, this book includes both poems by women, and the woman's voice as interpreted by male writers. The female voice is more abundant in recent writing than that of past centuries.

Curiously, directness of language and succinctness of phrasing, common to the language of poetry at the beginning of the twenty-first century, as in the lines from John Montague, is most frequently paralleled by the terse and elegant poems of the ninth and subsequent centuries, showing a return to language that is as refined as it is economical. In translation, the cryptic Irish original often displays a remarkable concision, lacking in the English version:

Cride hé,
daire cnó,
ócán é,
pócán dó.

Such a heart!
Should he leave, how I'd miss him.
Jewel, acorn, youth.
Kiss him!

Anon, 'A Love Song', 9th–10th century,
translated by Frank O'Connor

The vast bedroom
a hall of air,
our linked bodies
lying there.

John Montague, 'Tracks'

The themes under which the poems are arranged begin with poetic dialogues between couples. The delightful question-and-answer session between an early eighteenth-century couple, Seán Ó Neachtain and Úna Ní Bhroin, has the spirit of affectionate and intimate communication between familiars, with the birdlife of the woods as their natural habitat. Such harmony is contrasted by the couple in 'The Volatile Kerryman', where the man is opportunistic, the woman deluded by his false promises. Further exchanges are by turns humorous, melancholy or realistic with, in Paul Durcan's surreal 'My Belovèd Compares Herself to a Pint of Stout', the imagery of drinking assuming unexpected connotations.

Declarations follow – expressions of love, or its denial. Here lies the beginning and end of passion. The white heat of infatuation can express itself with wit, with subtlety, or with artistry, from the macaronic of 'O, how *bella*/Is my *Puella*' to 'Be still as you are beautiful' or 'You and I can mock the fabled wing, / For a kiss is an immortal thing', a conclusion to which most authors of love poems would agree. By contrast, the title 'On Not Being Your Lover' charts the aftermath.

Erotically charged poems are far less common than simple declarations of love or meditations on the complexity of relationships. A certain disdain hovers over many of the poems in this section. 'Glad to be out of her way, / Glad to rejoin her in bed', express a typical ambivalence that is mirrored by many writers, even those of the most powerfully expressed feelings, such as in E.R. Dodds' lines, 'And the world's shrunken to a heap, / Of hot flesh strained on a bed'. The erotic poems of Patrick Galvin are infused with a combination of directness and irony that is tinged with a tongue-in-cheek humour. The beauty of the female body is a central theme of love poetry; the male body by contrast has received scant poetic attention and is, in poetic terms, almost invisible. In Nuala Ní Dhomhnaill's poem on nudity, translated from the Irish by Paul Muldoon, the male body is celebrated as the poet exults in its physical perfection and allure:

Your skin so dark, my beloved,
and soft
as silk with a hint of velvet
in its weft,

smelling as it does of meadowsweet
or 'watermead'
that has the power, or so it's said,
to drive men and women mad.

Nuala Ní Dhomhnaill, 'Nude'

Nude Study (1906)
William Orpen (1878–1931)

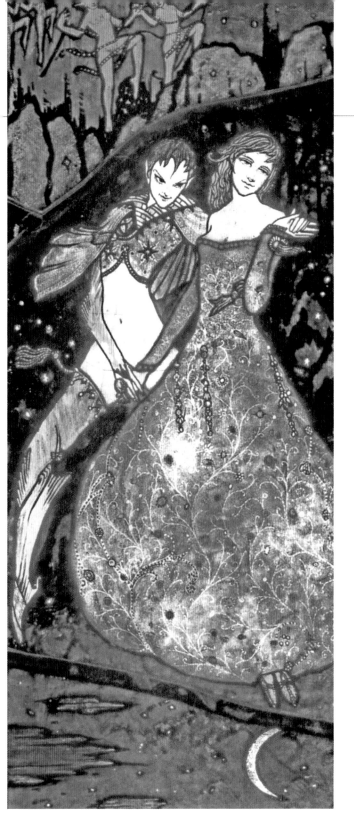

From the late seventeenth century, Séathrún Céitinn, in his poem 'Dear Woman with your Wiles', writes in a tone that is reflected more recently in the poems of Patrick Galvin, about the physical failings of the aging male. Two hundred years after Céitinn, Thomas Moore treats the same topic with a more sprightly grace.

Relationships are at the core of much poetry, whether the topic is love or any other aspect of engagement. Esther Johnson, the 'Stella' of Jonathan Swift's writing, was much perturbed on discovering the Dean's relationship with a younger woman, Esther Vanhomrigh, for whom Swift had coined the name 'Vanessa'. Johnson's short poem 'On Jealousy' expresses the pain of feeling that there is a rival for the affections of her beloved. L.A.G. Strong in 'The Brewer's Man' is unequivocal in depicting with humour a relationship gone wrong, a brief vignette but evocative of a whole world of hazardous encounters. In 'The Globe in Carolina' Derek Mahon elegantly sets a scene where, across continents, the distant lover is remembered: the relationship is sustained by the mere act of recollection.

The mundane is the theme of domestic love, the tactile significance and beauty of small things, the emotion that can be startlingly evoked by objects and by rituals. In Seamus Heaney's sensuous description of a wild animal, 'black, striped and damasked like a chasuble', he transmutes this striking image into a recollection of his own beloved, delving into a clothes drawer, while in 'Na hEallaí' by Macdara Woods, the ritualistic tasks of putting a house in order for departure become the catalyst for recalling the absent one, the 'you' of the poem.

The trials of troubled love have generated as many, if not more poems than verses devoted to harmonious relationships. Toirdhealbach Ó Cearbhalláin (Turlough O'Carolan), a close contemporary of Jonathan Swift, is celebrated for his harp music dedicated to aristocratic patrons, rather than for his poetry, yet in 'Betty O'Brien', translated by Ireland's first president, the noted Irish language scholar, Douglas Hyde, he voices the frustrated desires of many, a refrain found throughout all Irish love poetry, over many hundreds of years: all he yearns for is a kiss! And then there is 'The Midnight Court', Brian Merriman's masterpiece of sexual frustration that charts women's dissatisfaction with male behaviour – their reluctance to make commitments, to marry – with clerical celibacy and with the marriage of young girls to grotesque elderly men. These and many more arguments of the gender war confirm that sexual dynamics are as ageless as life itself.

The Dreamers, The Geneva Window
Harry Clarke (1889–1931)

Ambivalence, to be found in the work of many poets, finds a powerful expression in Alice Furlong's alternating verses of love/hate:

> I would lift you to the skies,
> I would give you paradise;
> I would suffer Hell's worst dole
> For the saving of your soul.
>
> *Wounding coldness to reprove*
> *I would wound you in my love.*
> *Suppliant still at your heart's gate*
> *I do worship in my hate.*
>
> Alice Furlong, 'To the Beloved'

There are many fine poems evoking passionate love for those who have died, wives and lovers, love either consummated or not. The thirteenth-century elegy, 'On the Death of His Wife' by Muireadhach Albanach Ó Dálaigh, is among the finest in the almost tactile directness and immediacy of its description of the poet's loss. The anonymous 'I am Stretched on Your Grave', from the eighteenth century, expresses a similar despair for love lost. Also from the late eighteenth century, in the 'Lament for Art O'Leary', Eibhlin Dubh Ní Chonnaill, a young widow, expresses her anger, loss and despair at the death of her murdered husband, in a language that is both a traditional mourning refrain and a personally passionate response to bereavement. The melancholy of love lost in James Joyce's most famous short story 'The Dead' is echoed in a lamentation in which communication continues after death:

> Rain on Rahoon falls softly, softly falling,
> Where my dark lover lies.
> Sad is his voice that calls me, sadly calling,
> At grey moonrise.
>
> James Joyce, 'She Weeps Over Rahoon'

The poetry of the early twenty-first century is more often preoccupied with sorrow than joy. In a love poem of spectacular bleakness, Nick Laird adds a note of eroticism and violence to the depiction of attraction. In this mini-drama of a life cut short, the reader's imagination must fill in the sparse narrative.

> I am not a good man
> into my grave into my grave into my grave she was laid.
>
> Nick Laird, 'Lust'

Le Mort du Cygne: Anna Pavlova (1911)
John Lavery (1856–1941)

DIALOGUES

A Dinner of Herbs
George William Joy (1844–1925)

Give me, my love, that billing kiss

ORDEAL BY COHABITATION

Anon (7th–12th century)

HE

    So I and my love Liadain

    Should sleep together without sin

    While any layman on the earth

    Would boast of what that chance was worth,

SHE

    Though I and my love Cuirither

    Had practised virtue for a year,

    Left together for one night

    Our thoughts would stray before daylight.

Translated by Frank O'Connor

Early Morning (1922)
William Orpen (1878–1931)

PROPOSAL TO ÚNA NÍ BHROIN

Seán Ó Neachtain

Glad I'd go to the wood with you, girl of the gold curls
and see the birds there in sweet-throated session:
the nightingale will play fiddle, the thrush a whistle
the blackbird accompany himself on the harp,

his dun mate on the organ, the wren wake a lute
the laverock and titmouse on tabor and snare.
Parked on a green bough, the trumpeter sparrow
will strike up a hot number all for your love.

Woodpigeon and turtle will chortle together
starling and fieldfare trotting nearby
the cuckoo will seek just one shy keek
of you, and the corncrake's your boon friend.

Echoes at our shoulders relay merry laughter
women from the raths and the mounds ply their strings
everything you could think to wish for, my minx,
is yours, and my love will never depart you.

Daylight will drench us, down through the branches
orient drops upon them sparkle and play
you the chattering music of water, while the otter
and the fish writhe together, intricately.

Translated by Kit Fryatt

Longlanguish
Michael Canning (1971–)

REPLY TO SEÁN Ó NEACHTAIN'S PROPOSAL

Úna Ní Bhroin

From the time that I gave you my hand and my promise

And my love, too, forever, young Seán of the Neachtains

The advice of my friends could never divide us

— For you I'd abandon the halls of the angels.

Oh, love, a whole year I could go, I declare,

Without one bite of food or one round drop of drink,

My mouth on your mouth, love, and my hands in your hair

—Your love-talk would soon have us both in the pink.

I will leave with you now and will make no excuses

But will lie down and listen to the small birds at play

— One hundred times better than feasting in castles —

My firm love, my darling, how can I say Nay?

Translated by Patrick Crotty

Louisa Anna Molesworth (1771)
Hugh Douglas Hamilton (*c.*1734–1808)

THE VOLATILE KERRYMAN
Eoghan Rua Ó Súilleabháin

OWEN

I travelled the land from Leap to Corbally

From bright Glandore to sweet Roscarbery,

    Oh-roh! and to Cashel of sloes.

Fairs twice a week there on Thursday and Saturday,

High and low Masses there sung by the clergy,

Tankards and quarts full of wine and brandy,

Fine young women to keep you handy,

    Oh-roh! 'tis Heaven below.

GIRL

That would be the poor day if I ran away with you,

'Tis a rake of your like that would make me play with you,

    Oh-roh! 'Twould be madness to go!

Oh, my father won't mind if you say you'll marry me,

But he'll murder us both if to Kerry you carry me,

    Oh-roh! with a terrible blow.

But if you give your oath that you'll never stray from me

I'll buy you strong drink that will coax you to stay with me.

Make up your mind and say you'll come home with me,

  (Coaxing)

Make up your mind and say you'll come home with me,

    Oh-roh! And my fortune you'll own.

OWEN

Oh, there's no place on earth that I wouldn't go with you,

And I'd fit out a ship if I thought 'twould pleasure you,

    Oh-roh! O'er the ocean we'd go.

I would carry you with me across to Germany,

In Venice or Rome we'd have wine and company,

Come and be brave! Don't be afraid of me!

    (Coaxing)

Come and be nice, and travel away with me.

    Oh-roh! my darling, my own.

GIRL

Oh, I'd travel the world and Newfoundland with you,

And to see foreign countries would surely be grand with you,

    Oh-roh! 'tis happy I'd go.

But to wed me your promise I must be certain of,

And to live out our lives in sweet contentment, love,

    Oh-roh! 'tis you I adore.

OWEN

Here is my hand in your hand to hold with you,

To bind us for life so that I'll grow old with you,

Our engagement is made now, and love in my heart for you,

There's a half of my soul that will never part from you.

    Oh-roh! while the world shall roll.

Portrait of a Young Man (1945)
Patrick Hennessy (1915–1980)

GIRL

If I follow you close to the slopes of Carbery,

My senses I'll lose if you don't come home with me,

    Oh-roh! the teardrops will flow.

OWEN

Bring a purseful of gold for the road along with you,

For money's no load when 'tis golden sovereigns,

    Oh-roh! to spend as we roam.

GIRL

Your hands will be soft without trace of work on them

No digging potatoes or cutting turf with them,

OWEN

There'll be dancing all night, and drinking and

    devilment;

GIRL

Music and whiskey,

OWEN

    For money makes merriment,

BOTH

    Oh-roh! 'tis the Devil's own sport.

GIRL

But you're telling me lies, you don't mean the half of it,

Coaxing me now, and in a while you'll laugh at it,

    Oh-roh! 'Twould make me a show.

OWEN

Oh love of my heart, my dear, pay heed to me,

I wouldn't deceive you for Ireland free to me.

For fear it would lead me to Hell's black deanery,

Sweet and dear will you always be to me,

    Oh-roh! 'til in the coffin I go.

GIRL

Don't mention the coffin, bad luck to speak of it,

But talk of fine sport for 'tis we'll be seeking it,

    Oh-roh! and adventures galore!

Call in the neighbours, there's barrels of porter full

And we'll make a great noise will be heard in Waterford.

    Oh-roh! while the world shall roll!

Oh, I'd rather your love than the riches of Solomon,

Acres of cattle or valleys of singing birds,

I've made up my mind, and the Pope couldn't

    change it now,

I'd give you the world if I could arrange it now.

    Oh-roh! my darling, my own!

OWEN

A fortnight spent travelling far and wide with her,
Making up songs for her, telling lies to her,
    Oh-roh! to keep her aglow,
'Til the last golden sovereign I winkled out of her,
Sweetly and easily, never a shout from her,
    Oh-roh! indeed money's no load!
Oh, 'twas smartly I settled my beaver hat on me,
The blackthorn stick and the coat that flattered me,
And over the ditches I fled like a bat from her,
Home to Kerry, like a scalded cat from her,
    Oh-roh! while she trotted below

As nightfall came on, she was most astonished
To see that her darling had totally vanished —
    Oh-roh! with a great hullagone!
She tore at her hair like a raving lunatic,
She swore I betrayed her and fairly ruined her,

GIRL

    Oh-roh! He's gone with my gold.
Where is he now, oh where is that vagabond?
Make haste and be after him, carry him back to me,
That cursed rogue, that blathering Kerryman,
Breaking my heart with his rakish merriment,
    Oh-roh!

OWEN

    and it's goodbye to Owen!

Translated by Seán Ó Riada

THE COLLEEN RUE
Anon (18th–19th century)

As I roved out one summer's morning, speculating most curiously,
To my surprise, I soon espied a charming fair one approaching me;
I stood awhile in deep meditation, contemplating what should I do,
But recruiting all my sensations, I thus accosted the Colleen Rue:

'Are you Aurora, or the beauteous Flora, Euterpasia, or Venus bright?
Or Helen fair, beyond compare, that Paris stole from her
    Grecian's sight?
Thou fairest creature, you have enslaved me, I am intoxicated by
    Cupid's clue,
Whose golden notes and infatuation deranged my ideas for you,
    Colleen Rue.'

'Kind sir, be easy, and do not tease me, with your false praise so jestingly,
Your dissimulations and invitations, your fantastic praises, seducing me.
I am not Aurora, or the beauteous Flora, but a rural maiden to
    all men's view,
That's here condoling my situation, and my appellation is the Colleen Rue.'

'Was I Hector, that noble victor, who died a victim of Grecian skill,
Or was I Paris, whose deeds were various, as an arbitrator on Ida's Hill,
I would roam through Asia, likewise Arabia, through Pennsylvania
    seeking you,
The burning regions, like famed Vesuvius, for one embrace of the
    Colleen Rue.'

'Sir, I am surprised and dissatisfied at your tantalising insolence,

I am not so stupid, or enslaved by Cupid, as to be dupèd by your
eloquence,

Therefore desist from your solicitations, I am engaged, I declare it's true,

To a lad I love beyond all earthly treasures, and he'll soon embrace
his Colleen Rue.'

Tambourina (c.1820)
Adam Buck (1759–1833)

THE KISS

Thomas Moore

Give me, my love, that billing kiss
    I taught you one delicious night,
When, turning epicures in bliss,
    We tried inventions of delight.

Come, gently steal my lips along,
    And let your lips in murmurs move —
Ah, no! — again — that kiss was wrong —
    How can you be so dull, my love?

'Cease, cease!' the blushing girl replied —
    And in her milky arms she caught me —
'How can you thus your pupil chide;
    You know 'twas in the dark you taught me!'

The Falconer (1853)
Daniel Maclise (1806–1870)

ANY WIFE

Katharine Tynan

Nobody knows but you and I, my dear,

And the stars, the spies of God, that lean and peer,

Those nights when you and I in a narrow strait

Were under the ships of God and desolate.

In extreme pain, in uttermost agony,

We bore the cross for each other, you and I,

When, through the darkest hour, the night of dread,

I suffered and you supported my head.

Ties that bind us together for life and death,

O hard-set fight in the darkness, shuddering breath,

Because a man can only bear as he may,

And find no tears for easing, the woman's way,

Anguish of pity, sharp in the heart like a sword;

Dost Thou not know, O Lord? Thou knowest, Lord,

What we endured for each other: our wounds were red

When he suffered and I supported his head.

Grief that binds us closer than smile or kiss,

Into the pang God slips the exquisite bliss.

You were my angel and I your angel, as he,

The angel, comforted Christ in His agony,

Lifting Him up from the earth that His blood made wet,

Pillowing the Holy Head, dabbled in sweat,

Thou who wert under the scourges knowest to prove

Love by its pangs, love that endures for love.

Excelsior (1857)
Edward Sheil (1834–1866)

SHE BEING 78, HE BEING 84

Seán Ó Tuama

When they got married, we said
'They'll help to heat each other'
(she being 58, he being 64).
When he passed away we felt
bile rising in our mouths.

They had lived on dole and grants,
gossip their one solace —
but the dead face in the room now
was of an old king from the past.

She shrieked with rage, and combed him
with pagan fingerings
while we sound Christians prayed
that the lava-flow would stop.

She looked a widow of the Eastern world,
black shawl and moustached mouth,
the only woman in my lifetime
to have loved a prince
(she being 78, he being 84).

Mr and Mrs Thomas Haslam (1908)
Sarah Cecilia Harrison (1863–1941)

TÊTE À TÊTE

Thomas Kinsella

Try subtlety. 'I was in love all May
Not with you, really, but with You in Me.'

*Better a blunt avowal. Hour by hour
One wrong response contaminates the air.*

She loves … A web of doubt confused her sight
And silenced the window-table where they sat;

His fingers whitened on the trembling cup.
… *And I, as long as bantering passions keep.*

A complex wish to guide her altered to
A mild compunction as she poured his tea.

Their happiness when they forgave each other
Made neither ready to have faith in either.

Life is change and yields its deference
Not to good nor ill, but difference.

Last time they spoke it was of fumbled leaving;
The station deafening, the winter living.

The Consultation, 1917
William Sheehan (1894–1923)

MY BELOVÈD COMPARES HERSELF TO A PINT OF STOUT

Paul Durcan

When in the heat of the first night of summer
I observe with a whistle of envy
That Jackson has driven out the road for a pint of stout,
She puts her arm around my waist and scolds me:
Am I not your pint of stout? Drink me.
There is nothing except, of course, self-pity
To stop you also having your pint of stout.

Putting self-pity on a leash in the back of the car,
I drive out the road, do a U-turn,
Drive in the hall door, up the spiral staircase,
Into her bedroom. I park at the foot of her bed,
Nonchalantly step out leaving the car unlocked,
Stroll over to the chest of drawers, lean on it,
Circumspectly inspect the backs of my hands,
Modestly request from her a pint of stout.
She turns her back, undresses, pours herself into bed,
Adjusts the pillows, slaps her hand on the coverlet:
Here I am — at the very least
Look at my new cotton nightdress before you shred it
And do not complain that I have not got a head on me.

I look around to see her foaming out of the bedclothes
Not laughing but gazing at me out of four-leggèd eyes
She says: Close your eyes, put your hands around me.
I am the blackest, coldest pint you will ever drink
So sip me slowly, let me linger on your lips,
Ooze through your teeth, dawdle down your throat,
Before swooping down into your guts.

While you drink me I will deposit my scum
On your rim and when you get to the bottom of me,
No matter how hard you try to drink my dregs —
And being a man, you will, no harm in that —
I will keep bubbling up back at you.
For there is no escaping my aftermath.
Tonight — being the first night of summer —
You may drink as many pints of me as you like.
There are barrels of me in the tap room.
In thin daylight at nightfall,
You will fall asleep drunk on love.
When you wake early in the early morning
You will have a hangover,
All chaste, astringent, aflame with affirmation,
Straining at the bit to get to first mass
And holy communion and work — the good life.

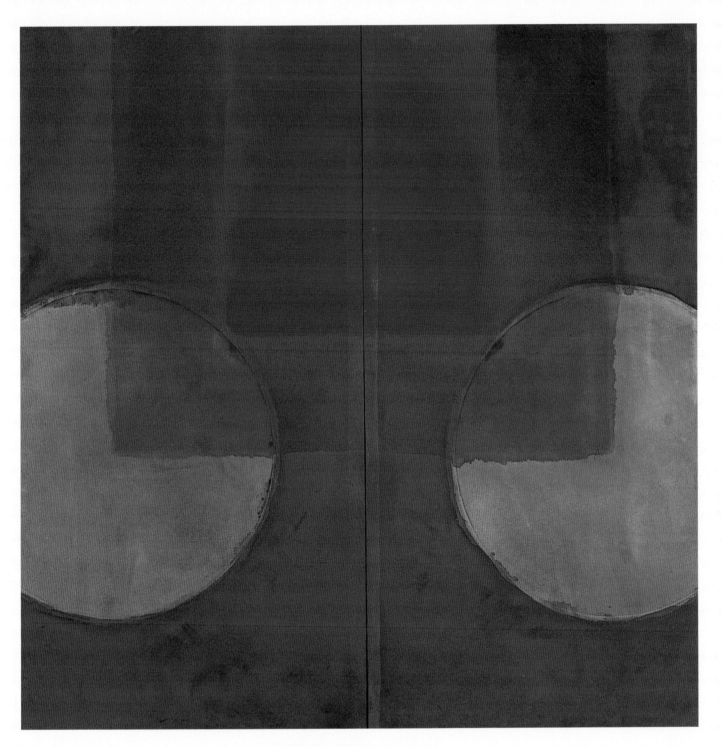

'Abstract' Diptych (1967)
Charles Tyrrell (1950–)

TWO SONGS FOR DOREEN

Derek Mahon

1 *His Song*

Months on, you hold me still;
at dawn, bright-rising, like a hill-
horizon, gentle, kind with rain
and the primroses of April.
I shall never know them again
but still your bright shadow
puts out its shadow, daylight, on
the shadows I lie with now.

2 *Her Song*

A hundred men imagine
love when I drink wine;
and then I begin to think
of your words and mine.
The mountain is silent now
where the snow lies fresh,
and my love like the sloe-
blossom on a blackthorn bush.

A Cry from the Mountain (1965)
Sean McSweeney (1935–)

LOVE DECLARED

On the Bridge at Grez (1884)
John Lavery (1856–1941)

 ——————————————————————————————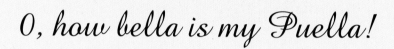

O, how bella is my Puella!

A LOVE SONG

Anon (9th–10th century)

Such a heart!

Should he leave, how I'd miss him.

Jewel, acorn, youth.

Kiss him!

Translated by Brendan Kennelly

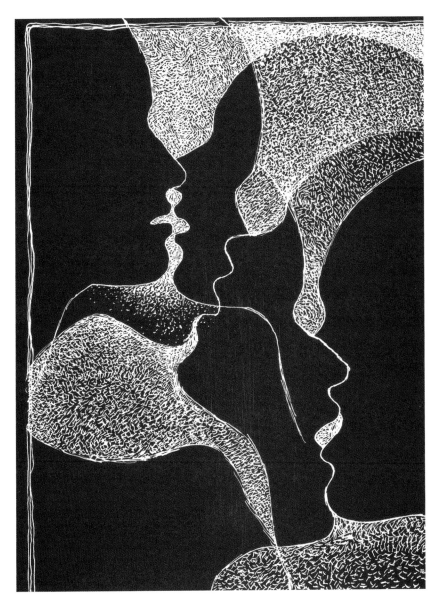

The Kiss, Inferno Canto V (2012)
Liam Ó Broin (1944–)

ON STELLA'S BIRTH-DAY

Jonathan Swift

Stella this Day is thirty four,

(We shan't dispute a Year or more)

However Stella, be not troubled,

Although thy Size and Years are doubled,

Since first I saw Thee at Sixteen

The brightest Virgin on the Green,

So little is thy Form declin'd

Made up so largely in thy Mind.

Oh, would it please the Gods to split

Thy Beauty, Size, and Years, and Wit,

No Age could furnish out a Pair

Of Nymphs so graceful, Wise and fair

With half the Lustre of Your Eyes,

With half your Wit, your Years and Size:

And then before it grew too late,

How should I beg of gentle Fate,

(That either Nymph might have her Swain,)

To split my Worship too in twain.

The Shepherdess (1914)
Harry Clarke (1889–1931)

Amo, Amas, I Love a Lass

John O'Keeffe

Amo, amas,
I love a lass
    As a cedar tall and slender;
Sweet cowslips' grace
Is her Nominative Case,
    And she's of the Feminine Gender.
    Rorum, corum, sunt Divorum,
        Harum, scarum Divo!
    Tag rag, merry derry, periwig and hatband,
        Hic hac, horum Genetivo!

Can I decline
A nymph divine?
    Her voice as a flute is *dulcis,*
Her *oculi* bright,
Her *manus* white,
    And soft, when I *tacto,* her pulse is!
    Rorum, corum, sunt Divorum,
        Harum scarum Divo!
    Tag rag, merry derry, periwig and hatband,
        Hic hac, horum Genetivo!

O, how *bella*
Is my *Puella!*
    I'll kiss *sæculorum!*
If I've luck, Sir,
She's my *Uxor* —
    O, dies benedictorum!
    Rorum, corum, sunt Divorum,
        Harum scarum Divo!
    Tag rag, merry derry, periwig and hatband,
        Hic, hac, horum Genetivo!

The Meeting on the Turret Stairs (1864)
Frederic William Burton (1816–1900)

Eileen Aroon
Gerald Griffin

When, like the early rose,
   Eileen aroon!
Beauty in childhood blows,
   Eileen aroon!
When, like a diadem,
Buds blush around the stem,
Which is the fairest gem?
   Eileen aroon!

Is it the laughing eye?
   Eileen aroon!
Is it the timid sigh?
   Eileen aroon!
Is it the tender tone,
Soft as the stringed harp's moan?
Oh! it is Truth alone,
   Eileen aroon!

When, like the rising day,
   Eileen aroon!
Love sends his early ray,
   Eileen aroon!
What makes his dawning glow
Changeless through joy or woe? —
Only the constant know,
   Eileen aroon!

I know a valley fair,
   Eileen aroon!
I knew a cottage there,
   Eileen aroon!

Far in that valley's shade
I knew a gentle maid,
Flower of a hazel glade,
   Eileen aroon!

Who in the song so sweet?
   Eileen aroon!
Who in the dance so fleet?
   Eileen aroon!
Dear were her charms to me,
Dearer her laughter free,
Dearest her constancy,
   Eileen aroon!

Youth must with time decay,
   Eileen aroon!
Beauty must fade away,
   Eileen aroon!
Castles are sacked in war,
Chieftains are scattered far,
Truth is a fixéd star,
   Eileen aroon!

Ballyneety II (2003)
Jack Donovan (1934–)

A WHITE ROSE

John Boyle O'Reilly

The red rose whispers of passion,
And the white rose breathes of love;
O, the red rose is a falcon,
And the white rose is a dove.

But I send you a cream-white rosebud,
With a flush on its petal tips;
For the love that is purest and sweetest
Has a kiss of desire on the lips.

*Cupid and Psyche in the
Nuptial Bower (1792)*
Hugh Douglas Hamilton (*c.*1734–1808)

HE GIVES HIS BELOVED CERTAIN RHYMES

W.B. Yeats

Fasten your hair with a golden pin,

And bind up every wandering tress;

I bade my heart build these poor rhymes:

It worked at them, day out, day in,

Building a sorrowful loveliness

Out of the battles of old times.

You need but lift a pearl-pale hand,

And bind up your long hair and sigh;

And all men's hearts must burn and beat;

And candle-like foam on the dim sand,

And stars climbing the dew-dropping sky,

Live but to light your passing feet.

Study for Ariadne (1907)
John Lavery (1856–1941)

I'D SWEAR FOR HER

James Doherty

I'd swear for her,
I'd tear for her,
The Lord knows what I'd bear for her;
I'd lie for her,
I'd sigh for her,
I'd drink Lough Erne dry for her;
I'd 'cuss' for her,
Do 'muss' for her,
I'd kick up a thundering fuss for her;
I'd weep for her,
I'd leap for her,
I'd go without any sleep for her;
I'd fight for her,
I'd bite for her,
I'd walk the streets all night for her;
I'd plead for her,
I'd bleed for her,
I'd go without my 'feed' for her;
I'd shoot for her,
I'd boot for her
A rival who'd come to 'suit' for her;

I'd kneel for her,
I'd steal for her,
Such is the love I feel for her;
I'd slide for her,
I'd ride for her,
I'd swim against wind and tide for her;
I'd try for her,
I'd cry for her,
But — hang me if I'd die for her
Or any other woman!

Portrait of Grace (1907)
William Orpen (1878–1931)

AFFINITY

George 'AE' Russell

You and I have found the secret way,
None can bar our love or say us nay:
All the world may stare and never know
You and I are twined together so.

You and I for all his vaunted width
Know the giant Space is but a myth;
Over miles and miles of pure deceit
You and I have found our lips can meet.

You and I have laughed the leagues apart
In the soft delight of heart to heart.
If there's a gulf to meet or limit set,
You and I have never found it yet.

You and I have trod the backward way
To the happy heart of yesterday,
To the love we felt in ages past.
You and I have found it still to last.

You and I have found the joy had birth
In the angel childhood of the earth,
Hid within the heart of man and maid.
You and I of Time are not afraid.

You and I can mock his fabled wing,
For a kiss is an immortal thing.
And the throb wherein those old lips met
Is a living muse in us yet.

Neighbours (2011)
Una Sealy (1959–)

BE STILL AS YOU ARE BEAUTIFUL

Patrick MacDonogh

Be still as you are beautiful,
    Be silent as the rose;
Through miles of starlit countryside
    Unspoken worship flows
To find you in your loveless room
    From lonely men whom daylight gave
The blessing of your passing face
    Impenetrably grave.

A white owl in the lichened wood
    Is circling silently,
More secret and more silent yet
    Must be your love to me.
Thus, while about my dreaming head
    Your soul in ceaseless vigil goes,
Be still as you are beautiful,
    Be silent as the rose.

Bon Voyage (1976)
Colin Middleton (1910–1983)

THREE GIFTS

Vincent Woods

I planted for you
The seventh tree of August
A white eucalyptus
In the red earth

I plucked for you
A flower from the desert
A blue miracle
In the hot sand

I named for you
The distance of the sun
A green lizard
In the world's eye

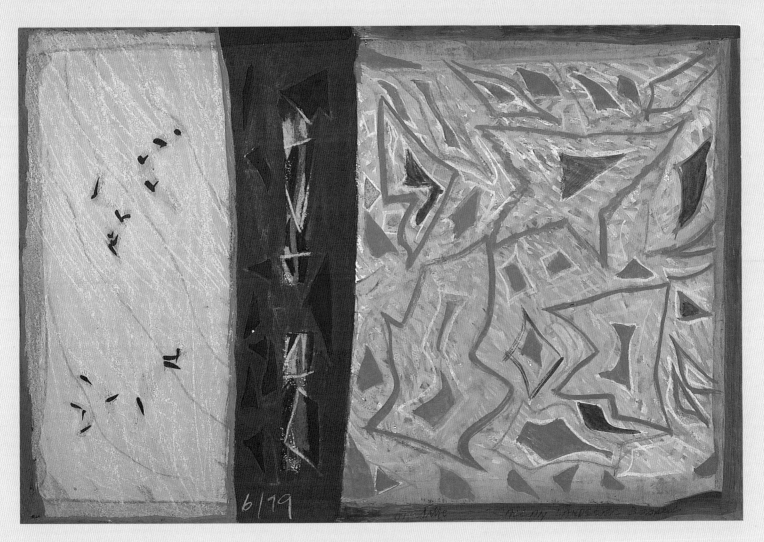

Callan Landscape, Three Aspects (1979)
Tony O'Malley (1913–2003)

THE GLASSHOUSE

Vona Groarke

It started with lapis lazuli,
an uncut nugget of blue-veined grey
that was your first gift to me.

Since then we have marked time or
love with stones like agate, quartz and amber,
which are, for us, just one way to remember.

For ten years, husband, we've been piling stones
and shifting them, in weighty bags, from one
place to another, and then home

to a house we wished on the lines of *amour
courtois* or happenstance, or some more
improbable stuff than bricks and mortar.

When we had nothing to speak of, we used stone.
Now that our house is set to dwell upon
a solid, shored-up bedrock of its own,

we think of it as bulk and not detail.
So what chance now for our bag of polished shale
to be turned out and worked into a trail

that would take us from our first word
to our last, if it has been said or heard,
in the here and now of language almost shared?

The Headland (1993)
William Crozier (1930–2011)

I could say that one is glazed with rain
the way your hand was when you wrote your name
and number in my book that Saturday.

Or that one has the smoothness of your cheek,
that one is dimpled like the small of your back,
or that one is freckled like your sunburned neck.

I could say that there is one which is warm,
as though you had been holding it in the palm
of your hand, a while before I came;

that one is perfect as the white of your eye,
and that there is one which I think may
just remind you, afterwards, of me;

that the hilt of one could hurt us,
or pierce the walls of a delicate house
that, in the end, may be as breakable as glass.

But it cannot slip from your hand or
from my own, my love, not now, when our
stones that we picked in time are thrown asunder

on Ballagan Point, where we stood lately, side by side
with stones in our pockets and stones in our hands,
to promise each other the sky, and its blue-veined clouds.

LOVE DENIED

The Green Sofa (1908)

John Lavery (1856–1941)

When I go by myself to the Well of Loneliness

I WILL NOT DIE FOR YOU

Anon (17th century)

I will not die for you,
    lady with swanlike body.
Meagre men you have killed so far,
    and not the likes of me.

For what would make me die?
    Lips of red, or teeth like blooms?
A gentle hand, a lime-white breast?
    Should I die for these?

Your cheerful mood, your noble mind?
    O slender palm and flank like foam,
eye of blue and throat of white,
    I will not die for you.

Your rounded breasts, O skin refined,
    your flushed cheeks, your waving hair
— certainly I will not die
    on their account, unless God will.

Your narrow brows, your hair like gold,
    your chaste intent, your languid voice,
your smooth calf, your curved heel
    — only meagre men they kill.

Lady with swanlike body,
    I was reared by a cunning hand!
I know well how women are.
    I will not die for you.

Self-Portrait
Daniel Maclise (1806–1870)

MY LOVE IS LIKE THE SUN

Anon (18th century)

The winter is past,
And the summer's come at last
And the blackbirds sing in every tree;
The hearts of these are glad
But my poor heart is sad,
For my true love is parted from me.

The rose upon the briar
By the water running clear
Gives joy to the linnet and the bee;
Their little hearts are blest
But mine is not at rest,
Since my true love is absent from me.

A livery I'll wear
And I'll comb out my hair,
And in velvet so green I will appear,
And straight I will repair
To the Curragh of Kildare
For it's there I'll find tidings of my dear.

I'll wear a cap of black
With a frill around my neck,
Gold rings on my fingers I will wear:
And this I'll undertake
All for my true love's sake,
Who resides at the Curragh of Kildare.

I would not think it strange
The whole wide world to range
In search of tidings of my dear;
But here in Cupid's chain
I am bound to remain,
And to spend my whole life in despair.

My love is like the sun
That in the firmament does run,
And always proves constant and true;
But he is like the moon
That wanders up and down,
The moon that every month is new.

All ye that are in love
And cannot it remove,
I pity the pains you endure;
For experience lets me know
That your hearts are full of woe,
A woe that no mortal can cure.

The Unread Vision (2008)
Margaret Egan (*c*.1950–)

DÓNAL ÓG

Anon (18th–19th century)

It is late last night the dog was speaking of you;
the snipe was speaking of you in her deep marsh.
It is you are the lonely bird through the woods;
and that you may be without a mate until you find me.

You promised me, and you said a lie to me,
that you would be before me where the sheep are
  flocked;
I gave a whistle and three hundred cries to you,
and I found nothing there but a bleating lamb.

You promised me a thing that was hard for you,
a ship of gold under a silver mast;
twelve towns with a market in all of them,
and a fine white court by the side of the sea.

You promised me a thing that is not possible,
that you would give me gloves of the skin of a fish;
that you would give me shoes of the skin of a bird;
and a suit of the dearest silk in Ireland.

When I go by myself to the Well of Loneliness,
I sit down and I go through my trouble;
when I see the world and do not see my boy,
he that has an amber shade in his hair.

It was on that Sunday I gave my love to you;
the Sunday that is last before Easter Sunday.
And myself on my knees reading the Passion;
and my two eyes giving love to you for ever.

My mother said to me not to be talking with you today,
or tomorrow, or on the Sunday;
it was a bad time she took for telling me that;
it was shutting the door after the house was robbed.

My heart is as black as the blackness of the sloe,
or as the black coal that is on the smith's forge;
or as the sole of a shoe left in white halls;
it was you put that darkness over my life.

You have taken the east from me; you have taken the west
  from me;
you have taken what is before me and what is behind me;
you have taken the moon, you have taken the sun from me
and my fear is great that you have taken God from me!

Translated by Lady Augusta Gregory

Owl With Oak Leaves (1972)
Edward McGuire (1932–1986)

THE OUTLAW OF LOCH LENE

Jeremiah Joseph Callanan

O many a day have I made good ale in the glen,

That came not of stream, or malt, like the brewing of men.

My bed was the ground, my roof the greenwood above,

And the wealth that I sought — one far kind glance from my love.

Alas! on that night when the horses I drove from the field,

That I was not near from terror my angel to shield.

She stretched forth her arms — her mantle she flung to the wind,

And swam o'er Loch Lene, her outlawed lover to find.

O would that a freezing sleet-winged tempest did sweep,

And I and my love were alone far off on the deep!

I'd ask not a ship, or a bark, or pinnace to save, —

With her hand round my waist, I'd fear not the wind or the wave.

'Tis down by the lake where the wild tree fringes its sides,

The maid of my heart, the fair one of Heaven resides —

I think as at eve she wanders its mazes along,

The birds go to sleep by the sweet wild twist of her song.

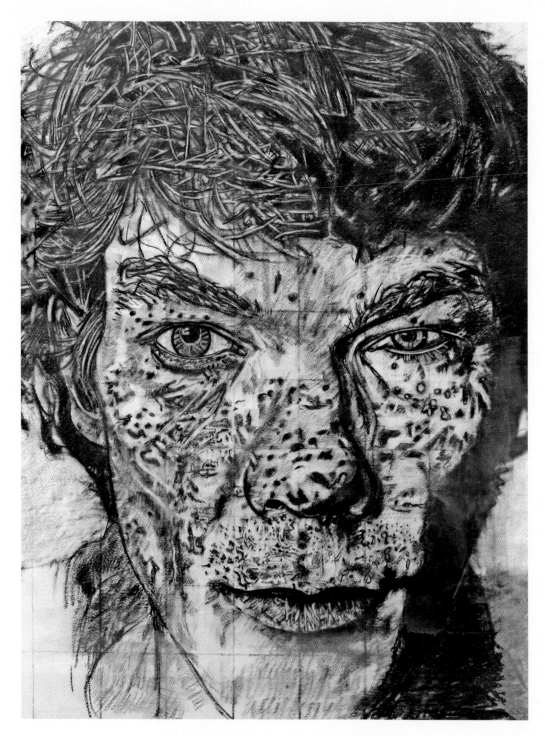

Drawing of a Man (2006)
Gary Coyle (1965–)

NO SECOND TROY

W.B. Yeats

Why should I blame her that she fill my days

With misery, or that she would of late

Have taught to ignorant men most violent ways,

Or hurled the little streets upon the great,

Had they but courage equal to desire?

What could have made her peaceful with a mind

That nobleness made simple as a fire,

With beauty like a tightened bow, a kind

That is not natural in an age like this,

Being high and solitary and most stern?

Why, what could she have done, being what she is?

Was there another Troy for her to burn?

'A Fair Spaniard', A Portrait of Mrs Chowne
John Lavery (1856–1941)

ON RAGLAN ROAD

Patrick Kavanagh

On Raglan Road on an autumn day I met her first and knew

That her dark hair would weave a snare that I might
    one day rue;

I saw the danger, yet I walked along the enchanted way,

And I said, let grief be a fallen leaf at the dawning of
    the day.

On Grafton Street in November we tripped lightly along
    the ledge

Of the deep ravine where can be seen the worth of
    passion's pledge,

The Queen of Hearts still making tarts and I not making
    hay —

O I loved too much and by such by such is happiness
    thrown away.

I gave her gifts of the mind, I gave her the secret sign
    that's known

To the artists who have known the true gods of sound
    and stone

And word and tint. I did not stint for I gave her poems
    to say.

With her own name there and her own dark hair like
    clouds over fields of May.

On a quiet street where old ghosts meet I see her
  walking now
Away from me so hurriedly my reason must allow
That I had wooed not as I should a creature made of
  clay —
When the angel wooes the clay he'd lose his wings at
  the dawn of day.

While You Were Out (2001)
Andrew Folan (1956–)

ON NOT BEING YOUR LOVER

Medbh McGuckian

Your eyes were ever brown, the colour
Of time's submissiveness. Love nerves
Or a heart, beat in their world of
Privilege, I had not yet kissed you
On the mouth.

But I would not say, in my un-freedom
I had weakly drifted there, like the
Bone-deep blue that visits and decants
The eyes of our children:

How warm and well-spaced their dreams
You can tell from the sleep-late mornings
Taken out of my face! Each lighted
Window shows me cardiganed, more desolate
Than the garden, and more hallowed
Than the hinge of the brass-studded
Door that we close, and no one opens,
That we open and no one closes.

In a far-flung, too young part,
I remembered all your slender but
Persistent volume said, friendly, complex
As the needs of your new and childfree girl.

Home After Work (1863)
Edward Sheil (1834–1866)

Eros

Man and Poppies (1981)
Pauline Bewick (1935–)

And lips are crushed on hot blind lips

ADVICE TO LOVERS

Anon (7th–12th century)

The way to get on with a girl
Is to drift like a man in a mist;
Happy enough to be caught,
Happy to be dismissed.

Glad to be out of her way,
Glad to rejoin her in bed,
Equally grieved or gay
To learn that she's living or dead.

Translated by Frank O'Connor

Jou Jou (1939)
Colin Middleton (1910–1983)

POLITICS

W.B. Yeats

*'In our time the destiny of man presents its meanings in
political terms:' — Thomas Mann*

How can I, that girl standing there,

My attention fix

On Roman or on Russian

Or on Spanish politics,

Yet here's a travelled man that knows

What he talks about,

And there's a politician

That has both read and thought,

And maybe what they say is true

Of war and war's alarms,

But O that I were young again

And held her in my arms.

Portrait of My Daughter Michelle (2008)
Carey Clarke (1936–)

WHEN THE ECSTATIC BODY GRIPS

E.R. Dodds

When the ecstatic body grips
Its heaven, with little sobbing cries,
And lips are crushed on hot blind lips,
I read strange pity in your eyes.

For that in you which is not mine,
And that in you which I love best,
And that, which my day-thoughts divine
Masterless still, still unpossessed,

Sits in the blue eyes' frightened stare,
A naked lonely-dwelling thing,
A frail thing from its body-lair
Drawn at my body's summoning;

Whispering low, 'O unknown man,
Whose hunger on my hunger wrought,
Body shall give what body can,
Shall give you all — save what you sought.'

Whispering, 'O secret one, forgive,
Forgive and be content though still
Beyond the blood's surrender live
The darkness of the separate will.

'Enough if in the veins we know
Body's delirium, body's peace —
Ask not that ghost to ghost shall go,
Essence in essence may cease.'

But swiftly, as in sudden sleep,
That You in you is veiled or dead;
And the world's shrunken to a heap
Of hot flesh strained on a bed.

The Forest Pool (1946)
Nano Reid (1905–1981)

THE NEGLECTED WIFE

Patrick Galvin

Look, woman,
Go away from me.
I do not want you in my bed
My feather bed with the four posters.
Besides, you are a married woman
With a poet for a husband
And I cannot renege
On a fellow-artist.

Don't tempt me.
It is true I have done it before —
My reputation haunts me.
But I was young then
And bloated with lechery.
Now my blood is like ice
And my mind is on holier things
Than a woman's genitals.

Laugh, if you will
But I'm tired of such nonsense.
To-day, I can walk in the streets
With a fine conscience
Knowing I am safe from all harm
By demented husbands and distracted lovers.
The pleasures of old age
Are more than fabulous.

True, if I were young again
And flesh-tormented
I might desire you greatly.
Your belly is rapturous as snow
And your bottom staggers me
But that's by the way.
Control yourself now
And think how I've suffered.

I've had four husbands in my room
Shouting for my life
I've had lovers waiting on the stairs
To kick me on both shins.
No woman is worth such a sacrifice
And, you know, I no longer have the strength
Magnificent as you are
Lying there naked.

So remove yourself from my bed
And give my blessings to your husband —
But don't hurry yourself
Take time to dress.
And may Christ pardon me
This last fall.
It is an act of kindness
To a neglected wife.

Husbands and lovers
Do not condemn me
For the weakness in my loins
But pity me my lack of grace
And my poor upbringing
As God may pity you
In like circumstances.

Don Quixote's Penance Number Two (1970s)
Brian Bourke (1936–)

TRACKS
John Montague

I
The vast bedroom
a hall of air,
our linked bodies
lying there.

II
As I turn to kiss
your long, black
hair, small breasts,
heat flares from
your fragrant skin,
your eyes widen as
deeper, more certain
and often, I enter
to search possession
of where your being
hides in flesh.

III
Behind our eyelids
a landscape opens,
a violet horizon
pilgrims labour across,
a sky of colours
that change, explode
a fantail of stars
the mental lightning
of sex illuminating
the walls of the skull;
a floating pleasure dome.

IV
I shall miss you
creaks the mirror
into which the scene
shortly disappears:
the vast bedroom
a hall of air, the
tracks of our bodies
fading there, while
giggling maids push a
trolley of fresh
linen down the corridor.

Ocular Innocence (2008)
Diana Copperwhite (1969–)

NUDE

Nuala Ní Dhomhnaill

The long and short
of it is I'd far rather see you nude —
your silk shirt
and natty

tie, the brolly under your oxter
in case of a rainy day,
the three-piece seersucker
suit that's so incredibly trendy,

your snazzy loafers
and, la-di-da,
a pair of gloves
made from the skin of a doe,

then, to top it all, a crombie hat
set at a rak-
ish angle — none of these add
up to more than the icing on the cake.

For, unbeknownst to the rest
of the world, behind the outward
show lies a body unsurpassed
for beauty, without so much as a wart

or blemish, but the brill-
iant slink of a wild animal, a dream-
cat, say, on the prowl,
leaving murder and mayhem

in its wake. Your broad, sinewy
shoulders and your flank
smooth as the snow
on a snow-bank.

Your back, your slender waist,
and, of course,
the root that is the very seat
of pleasure, the pleasure-source.

Your skin so dark, my beloved,
and soft
as silk with a hint of velvet
in its weft,

smelling as it does of meadowsweet
or 'watermead'
that has the power, or so it's said,
to drive men and women mad.

For that reason alone, if for no other,
when you come with me to the dance tonight
(though, as you know, I'd much prefer
to see you nude)

it would probably be best
for you to pull on your pants and vest
rather than send
half the women of Ireland totally round the bend.

Translated by Paul Muldoon

Derval Standing I (2006)
Nick Miller (1962–)

A SONG

James Simmons

With your clothes on the chair
and one white sheet above you
I have no need of words
to explain why I love you.
Every touch of delight
through the long wedding night
Is defining our love.
With this kiss I thee wed.

If our luck should run out
and love withers and dies, love,
don't try out of kindness
to save me with this love
You won't need to explain
that I'm single again
and the marriage is done
when your kiss says goodbye.

Woman Seated at a Table (1951)
Stella Steyn (1907–1987)

YOUTH AND AGE

Youth and Age (1885)
John Lavery (1856–1941)

Against the victories of age

DEAR WOMAN, WITH YOUR WILES

Séathrún Céitinn

Dear woman, with your wiles,
You'd best remove your hand.
Though you burn with love's fire,
I'm no more an active man.

Look at the grey on my head,
See how my body droops,
Think of my sluggish blood —
What would you have me do?

It's not desire I lack.
Don't bend low like that again.
Love will live without the act
Forever, slender one.

Withdraw your lips from mine,
Strong as the inclination is,
Don't brush against my skin,
It could lead to wantonness.

The intricacy of curls,
Soft eyes clear as dew,
The pale sight of your curves,
Give pleasure to me now.

Bar what the body craves,
And lying with you requires,
I'll do for our love's sake,
Dear woman, with your wiles.

Translated by Maurice Riordan

Split Face I (1988)
Eithne Jordan (1954–)

BELIEVE ME, IF ALL THOSE ENDEARING YOUNG CHARMS

Thomas Moore

Believe me, if all those endearing young charms,
　　Which I gaze on so fondly today,
Were to change by to-morrow, and fleet in my arms,
　　Like fairy-gifts fading away!
Thou wouldst still be adored, as this moment thou art,
　　Let thy loveliness fade as it will,
And around the dear ruin, each wish of my heart
　　Would entwine itself verdantly still!

It is not while beauty and youth are thine own,
　　And thy cheeks unprofaned by a tear,
That the fervour and faith of a soul can be known,
　　To which time will but make thee more dear!

Oh! the heart that has truly loved never forgets
　　But as truly loves on to the close,
As the sun flower turns on her god, when he sets,
　　The same look which she turned when he rose!

Cherry Ripe (1860)
Jessie Douglas (*fl.*1893–1928)

WHEN YOU ARE OLD

W. B. Yeats

When you are old and grey and full of sleep,
And nodding by the fire; take down this book,
And slowly read, and dream of the soft look
Your eyes had once, and of their shadows deep;

How many loved your moments of glad grace,
And loved your beauty with love false or true,
But one man loved the pilgrim soul in you,
And loved the sorrows of your changing face;

And bending down beside the glowing bars,
Murmur, a little sadly, how Love fled
And paced upon the mountains overhead
And hid his face amid a crowd of stars.

Le Petit Déjeuner (1881)
Sarah Purser (1848–1943)

PLAISIR D'AMOUR
Patrick Galvin

SPRING

My father
Against the victories of age
Would not concede defeat,
He dyed his hair
And when my mother called
He said he wasn't there.

My mother, too
Fought back against the years
But in her Sunday prayers
Apologised to God.
My father said there was no God
'And that one knows it to her painted toes.'

My mother smiled.
She'd plucked her eyebrows too
And wore a see-through skirt
With matching vest.
'He likes French knickers best,' she said,
'I'll have them blest.'

My father raged.
He liked his women young, he said
And not half-dead.
He bought a second-hand guitar he couldn't play
And sang the only song he knew —
Plaisir d'amour.

SUMMER

When summer came
My father left the house.
He tied a ribbon in his hair
And wore a Kaftan dress.
My mother watched him walking down the street
'He'll break his neck in that,' she said —
'As if I care.'

He toured the world
And met a guru in Tibet.
'I've slept with women too,' he wrote,
'And they not half my age.'
My mother threw his letter in the fire —
'The lying gett — he couldn't climb the stairs
With all his years.'

She burned her bra
And wrote with lipstick on a card —
'I've got two sailors in the house
From Martinique.
They've got your children's eyes.'
My father didn't wait to answer that —
He came back home.

Your Turn (1986)
Jack Pakenham (1938–)

And sitting by the fire
He said he'd lied
He'd never slept with anyone but her.
My mother said she'd never lied herself —
She'd thrown the sailors out an hour before he came.
My father's heart would never be the same —
Plaisir d'amour.

AUTUMN

Through autumn days
My father felt the leaves
Burning in the corners of his mind.

My mother, who was younger by a year,
Looked young and fair.
The sailors from the port of Martinique
Had kissed her cheek.

He searched the house
And hidden in a trunk beneath the bed
My father found his second-hand guitar.
He found her see-through skirt
With matching vest.
'You wore French knickers once,' he said,
'I liked them best.'

'I gave them all away,' my mother cried,
'To sailors and to captains of the sea.
I'm not half-dead
'I'm fit for any bed — including yours.'
She wore a sailor's cap
And danced around the room
While father strummed his second-hand guitar.

He made the bed,
He wore his Kaftan dress,
A ribbon in his hair.
'I'll play it one more time,' he said,
'And you can sing.'
She sang the only song she knew —
Plaisir d'amour.

WINTER

At sixty-four
My mother died
At sixty-five
My father.

Comment from a neighbour
Who was there:
'They'd pass for twenty.'
Plaisir d'amour.

GOODBYE, SALLY

James Simmons

Shaken already, I know
I'll wake at night after you go
watching the soft shine of your skin,
feeling your little buttocks, oh my grief,
like two duck eggs in a handkerchief,
barely a woman but taking me all in.

I think our love won't die —
but there I go trying to justify!
What odds that we'll never meet again
and probably other girls will never
bring half your agony of pleasure?
Fidelity is a dumb pain.

God, but I'm lucky too,
the way I've muddled through
to ecstasy so often despite
exhaustion, drunkenness and pride.
How come that you were satisfied
and so was I that night?

It's true for drinker and lover,
the best stuff has no hangover.
You're right to spit on argument,
girl. Your dumbness on a walk
was better than my clown's talk.
You showed me what you meant.

Good mornings from every night
with you, thirsty and sore with appetite.
You never let me act my age.
Goodbye to all analysis and cause-
grubbing. The singer wants applause
not criticism as he leaves the stage.

Debs (2011)
Sheila Rennick (1983–)

CROSSING

John Montague

Your lithe and golden body
haunts me, as I haunt you:
corsairs with different freights
who may only cross by chance
    on lucky nights.

So our moorings differ.
But scents of your pleasure
still linger disturbingly
around me: fair winds or
    squalls of danger?

There is a way of forgetting you,
but I have forgotten it:
prepared wildly to cut free,
to lurch, like a young man,
    towards ecstasy!

Nightly your golden body turns
and turns in my shuddering dream.
Why is the heart never still,
yielding again to the cardinal
    lure of the beautiful?

Age should bring its wisdom
but in your fragrant presence
my truths are one, swirling
to a litany — sweet privateer —
    of grateful adulation.

John Anthony (2000)
Sean Scully (1945–)

RELATIONSHIPS

Peacocks in a Field
Mildred Anne Butler (1858–1941)

 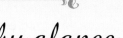

We'll know love little by little, glance by glance

STELLA'S BIRTH-DAY (March 13, 1726/7)

Jonathan Swift

This Day, whate'er the Fates decree,
Shall still be kept with Joy by me:
This Day then, let us not be told,
That you are sick, and I grown old,
Nor think on our approaching Ills,
And talk of Spectacles and Pills;
To morrow will be Time enough
To hear such mortifying Stuff.
Yet, since from Reason may be brought
A better and more pleasing Thought,
Which can in spite of all Decays,
Support a few remaining Days:
From not the gravest of Divines,
Accept for once some serious Lines.

Although we now can form no more
Long Schemes of Life, as heretofore;
Yet you, while Time is running fast,
Can look with Joy on what is past.

Were future Happiness and Pain,
A mere Contrivance of the Brain,
As Atheists argue, to entice,
And fit their Proselytes for Vice;
(The only Comfort they propose,
To have Companions in their Woes.)

Grant this the Case, yet sure 'tis hard,
That Virtue, stil'd its own Reward,
And by all Sages understood
To be the chief of human Good,
Should acting, die, nor leave behind
Some lasting Pleasure in the Mind,
Which by Remembrance will assuage,
Grief, Sickness, Poverty, and Age;
And Strongly shoot a radiant Dart,
To shine through Life's declining Part.

Say, *Stella,* feel you no Content,
Reflecting on a Life well spent?
Your skilful Hand employ'd to save
Despairing Wretches from the Grave;
And then supporting with your Store,
Those whom you dragg'd from Death before:
(So Providence on Mortals waits,
Preserving what it first creates)
Your gen'rous Boldness to defend
An innocent and absent Friend;
That Courage which can make you just,
To Merit humbled in the Dust:

Madeline After Prayer (1868)
Daniel Maclise (1806–1870)

The Detestation you express
For Vice in all its glitt'ring Dress:
That Patience under tort'ring Pain,
Where stubborn Stoicks would complain.

Shall these like empty Shadows pass,
Or Forms reflected from a Glass?
Or mere Chimæra's in the Mind,
That fly and leave no Marks behind?
Does not the Body thrive and grow
By Food of twenty Years ago?
And, had it not been still supply'd,
It must a thousand Times have dy'd.
Then, who with Reason can maintain,
That no Effects of Food remain?
And, is not Virtue in Mankind
The Nutriment that feeds the Mind?
Upheld by each good Action past,
And still continued by the last:
Then, who with Reason can pretend,
That all Effects of Virtue end?

Believe me *Stella*, when you show
That true Contempt for Things below,
Nor prize your Life for other Ends
Than merely to oblige your Friends;
Your former Actions claim their Part,
And join to fortify your Heart.
For Virtue in her daily Race,
Like *Janus*, bears a double Face;
Looks back with Joy where she has gone,
And therefore goes with Courage on.
She at your sickly Couch will wait,
And guide you to a better State.

O then, whatever Heav'n intends,
Take Pity on your pitying Friends;
Nor let your Ills affect your Mind,
To fancy they can be unkind.
Me, surely me, you ought to spare,
Who gladly would your Suff'rings share;
Or give my Scrap of Life to you,
And think it far beneath your Due;
You, to whose Care so oft I owe,
That I'm alive to tell you so.

ON JEALOUSY
Esther Johnson ('Stella')

O shield me from his rage, celestial powers!
This tyrant that embitters all my hours.
Ah, Love! you've poorly played the hero's part,
You conquered, but you can't defend my heart.
When first I bent beneath your gentle reign,

I thought this monster banished from your train:
But you would raise him to support your throne,
And now he claims your empire as his own;
Or tell me, tyrants, have you both agreed
That where one reigns, the other shall succeed?

The Wind (1995)
Donald Teskey (1956–)

HE REMEMBERS FORGOTTEN BEAUTY
W. B. Yeats

When my arms wrap you round I press
My heart upon the loveliness
That has long faded from the world;
The jewelled crowns that kings have hurled
In shadowy pools, when armies fled;
The love-tales wrought with silken thread
By dreaming ladies upon cloth
That has made fat the murderous moth;
The roses that of old time were
Woven by ladies in their hair,
The dew-cold lilies ladies bore
Through many a sacred corridor
Where such grey clouds of incense rose
That only God's eyes did not close:
For that pale breast and lingering hand
Come from a more dream-heavy land,
A more dream-heavy hour than this;
And when you sigh from kiss to kiss
I hear white Beauty sighing, too,
For hours when all must fade like dew,
But flame on flame, and deep on deep,
Throne over throne where in half sleep,
Their swords upon their iron knees,
Brood her high lonely mysteries.

Cassandra Fedele (1869)
Frederic William Burton (1816–1900)

BLUEBELLS FOR LOVE

Patrick Kavanagh

There will be bluebells growing under the big trees
And you will be there and I will be there in May;
For some other reason we both will have to delay
The evening in Dunshaughlin — to please
Some imagined relation,
So both of us came to walk through that plantation.

We will be interested in the grass,
In an old bucket-hoop, in the ivy that weaves
Green incongruity among dead leaves,
We will put on surprise at carts that pass —
Only sometimes looking sideways at the bluebells in the plantation
And never frighten them with too wild an exclamation.

We will be wise, we will not let them guess
That we are watching them or they will pose
A mere façade like boys
Caught out in virtue's naturalness.
We will not impose on the bluebells in that plantation
Too much of our desire's adulation.

We will have other loves — or so they'll think;
The primroses or the ferns or the briars,
Or even the rusty paling wires,
Or the violets on the sunless sorrel bank.
Only as an aside the bluebells in the plantation
Will mean a thing to our dark contemplation.

We'll know love little by little, glance by glance.

Ah, the clay under these roots is so brown!

We'll steal from Heaven while God is in the town —

I caught an angel smiling in a chance

Look through the tree-trunks of the plantation

As you and I walked slowly to the station.

Bluebell Woods
Sarah Walker (*c.*1960–)

MEETING POINT
Louis MacNeice

Time was away and somewhere else,
There were two glasses and two chairs
And two people with the one pulse
(Somebody stopped the moving stairs):
Time was away and somewhere else.

And they were neither up nor down;
The stream's music did not stop
Flowing through heather, limpid brown,
Although they sat in a coffee shop
And they were neither up nor down.

The bell was silent in the air
Holding its inverted poise —
Between the clang and clang a flower,
A brazen calyx of no noise:
The bell was silent in the air.

The camels crossed the miles of sand
That stretched around the cups and plates;
The desert was their own, they planned
To portion out the stars and dates:
The camels crossed the miles of sand.

Time was away and somewhere else.
The waiter did not come, the clock
Forgot them and the radio waltz
Came out like water from a rock:
Time was away and somewhere else.

Her fingers flicked away the ash
That bloomed again in tropic trees:
Not caring if the markets crash
When they had forests such as these,
Her fingers flicked away the ash.

God or whatever means the Good
Be praised that time can stop like this,
That what the heart has understood
Can verify in the body's peace
God or whatever means the Good.

Time was away and she was here
And life no longer what it was,
The bell was silent in the air
And all the room one glow because
Time was away and she was here.

Girl Reading (c.1910)
Roderic O'Conor (1860–1940)

THE BREWER'S MAN

L.A.G. Strong

Have I a wife? Bedam I have!
But we was badly mated.
I hit her a great clout one night
And now we're separated.

And mornin's going to me work
I meets her on the quay:
'Good mornin' to you, ma'am!' says I,
'To hell with ye!' says she.

Wicklow Labourer (1914)
Patrick Tuohy (1894–1930)

NIGHT DRIVE
Seamus Heaney

The smells of ordinariness
Were new on the night drive through France:
Rain and hay and woods on the air
Made warm draughts in the open car.

Signposts whitened relentlessly.
Montreuil, Abbeville, Beauvais
Were promised, promised, came and went,
Each place granting its name's fulfilment.

A combine groaning its way late
Bled seeds across its work-light.
A forest fire smouldered out.
One by one small cafés shut.

I thought of you continuously
A thousand miles south where Italy
Laid its loin to France on the darkened sphere.
Your ordinariness was renewed there.

Self-Portrait (2004)
Maeve McCarthy (1964–)

THE GLOBE IN CAROLINA

Derek Mahon

There are no religions, no revelations; there are women.
—Voznesensky, *Antiworlds*

The earth spins to my fingertips and
Pauses beneath my outstretched hand;
White water seethes against the green
Capes where the continents begin.
Warm breezes move the pines and stir
The hot dust of the piedmont where
Night glides inland from town to town.
I love to see that sun go down.

It sets in a coniferous haze
Beyond Georgia while the anglepoise
Rears like a moon to shed its savage
Radiance on the desolate page,
On Dvořàk sleeves and Audubon
Bird-prints; an electronic brain
Records the concrete music of
Our hardware in the heavens above.

From Hatteras to the Blue Ridge
Night spreads like ink on the unhedged
Tobacco fields and clucking lakes,
Bringing the lights on in the rocks
And swamps, the farms and motor courts,
Substantial cities, kitsch resorts —
Until, to the mild theoptic eye,
America is its own night-sky.

Out in the void and staring hard
At the dim stone where we were reared,
Great mother, now the gods have gone
We place our faith in you alone,
Inverting the procedures which
Knelt us to things beyond our reach.
Drop of the ocean, may your salt
Astringency redeem our fault!

Man Watching the Moon (2003)
Stephen McKenna (1939–)

Veined marble, if we only knew,
In practice as in theory, true
Redemption lies not in the thrust
Of action only, but the trust
We place in our peripheral
Night garden in the glory-hole
Of space, a home from home, and what
Devotion we can bring to it!

… You lie, an ocean to the east,
Your limbs composed, your mind at rest,
Asleep in a sunrise which will be
Your midday when it reaches me;
And what misgivings I might have
About the true importance of
The 'merely human' pale before
The mere fact of your being there.

Five miles away a southbound freight
Sings its euphoria to the state
And passes on; unfinished work
Awaits me in the scented dark.
The halved globe, slowly turning, hugs
Its silence, while the lightning bugs
Are quiet beneath the open window,
Listening to that lonesome whistle blow …

YEARN ON
Katie Donovan

I want you to feel
the unbearable lack of me.
I want your skin
to yearn for the soft lure of mine;
I want those hints of red
on your canvas
to deepen in passion for me:
carmine, burgundy.
I want you to keep
stubbing your toe
on the memory of me;
I want your head to be dizzy
and your stomach in a spin;
I want you to hear my voice
in your ear, to touch your face
imagining it is my hand.
I want your body to shiver and quiver
at the mere idea of mine.

Bert, the Big Foot,
sung by Villon
Harry Clarke (1889–1931)

I want you to feel as though
life after me is dull, and pointless,
and very, very aggravating;
that with me you were lifted
on a current you waited all your life to find,
and had despaired of finding,
as though you were wading
through a soggy swill of inanity and ugliness
every minute we are apart.
I want you to drive yourself crazy
with the fantasy of me,
and how we will meet again, against all odds,
and there will be tears and flowers,
and the vast relief of not I,
but us.
I am haunting your dreams,
conducting these fevers
from a distance,
a distance that leaves me weeping,
and storming,
and bereft.

DOMESTIC LOVE

Old John's Cottage, Connemara (1908)
William Orpen (1878–1931)

Your palms smooth as a washed baking-board

SONG FOR STRAPHANGERS

George Buchanan

I bought a red-brick villa
  and dug the garden round
because a young girl smiled in June:
  in August we were bound
    by a marriage vow,
    and then till now
I count up every pound.

I count up every penny,
  I work and never cease,
because a young girl smiled in June
  and there is no release.
    Sometimes I swear
    it's most unfair.
Sometimes I feel at peace.

River to the Sea (1959)
Norah McGuinness (1901–1980)

THE SKUNK

Seamus Heaney

Up, black, striped and damasked like the chasuble
At a funeral mass, the skunk's tail
Paraded the skunk. Night after night
I expected her like a visitor.

The refrigerator whinnied into silence.
My desk light softened beyond the verandah.
Small oranges loomed in the orange tree.
I began to be tense as a voyeur.

After eleven years I was composing
Love-letters again, broaching the word 'wife'
Like a stored cask, as if its slender vowel
Had mutated into the night earth and air

Of California. The beautiful, useless
Tang of eucalyptus spelt your absence.
The aftermath of a mouthful of wine
Was like inhaling you off a cold pillow.

And there she was, the intent and glamorous,
Ordinary, mysterious skunk,
Mythologized, demythologized,
Snuffing the boards five feet beyond me.

It all came back to me last night, stirred
By the sootfall of your things at bedtime,
Your head-down, tail-up hunt in a bottom drawer
For the black plunge-line nightdress.

Chanteuse (2006)
Brian Bourke (1936–)

Na hEallaí

Macdara Woods

This is my ship
and the storm outside is you

all of you — and absence
irregular bursts of thunder

again I close the shutters
open them

throw logs on the fire
and wonder at the early dark

Tonight
I must wash the floors

tomorrow strip the bed
turn off the water

in the pipes — pack my bags
and leave again

Five days now I've been
imprisoned

with that ambivalent
pronoun *you* —

that signifies presence
absence silence

do *you* remember
reading to me

for the sick and dying
in the black-bound

Book of
Common Prayer

to comfort me keep me
from drowning

in delirium
being lost in absence

Until now: and the only *you*
I can speak to

is absence is silence
is silence is distance

is absence is distance
is you

Still Life – Leeks and Red Cabbage (2006)
Geraldine O'Neill (1971–)

THE SMELL OF CAKE

Seán Dunne

I love the smell of cake in kitchens,
To stand in the heat of work and feel
The air warm as baked stones.
Dough clings to wooden spoons and bowls,
The worn edges of an old recipe book.
And your hair is powdered with flour,
Your palms smooth as a washed baking-board.
Above all, I love the finish when, together
Under the calendar that's months behind,
We swop spoons from a basin of cream and lick,
My beard flecked with it, your chin white,
And between us our son yelling for a lick,
And rising all around, the smell of rich, cooked cake.

Polythene Wrapped Turf Stack and an
Egg Broken on a Pan (1975)
T.P. Flanagan (1929–2011)

TROUBLED LOVE

Composition with Three Elements (c.1935)
Mainie Jellett (1897–1944)

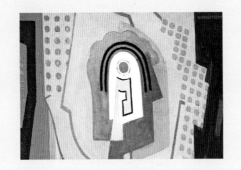

I would leave you in sore want

BEITÍ NÍ BHRIAIN (BETTY O'BRIEN)

Toirdhealbhach Ó Cearbhalláin / Turlough O'Carolan

There is a stately woman of Munster,

Nigh unto the Boyne,

   As each good learned-man says,

She is Betty O'Brian,

The maiden of the locks,

   The girl of most lovely laugh,

How is it worth while for me to be alive

Unless I shall get a kiss

   From her mouth like a rose in a garden?

I myself assert it to you

That if she were in Egypt

   I would go to look at her beauty.

The mild woman, sunny, shapely,

   The sister of O'Brian and MacCarthy,

Whosoever would sit by her side

And would kiss her mouth,

   Life and health were near to him.

I placed delight

In the back of ringlets,

   By which I have lost activity and health.

Sleep in the night

I do not get for want of her,

Without my being constantly near her.

Oh, Betty of the mild eyes,

Who hast led astray every province,

  You, with whom the thousands are in love,

The riches of Greece

I would not accept at all

  If I got my choice of being betrothed to you,

Oh, plant of the true blood

And sister of kings,

  With whom the world is in love and affection,

How you are like to Deirdre,

Oh, darling of the women of Erin,

  Oh, lily, who won the victory for loveliness.

Oh, sister of the secret

Do not do that,

  But with the inclining of your eye give me relief,

Keep me from the death,

Let you yourself have me,

  And I shall be merry and pleased.

The county of Leitrim of the welcomes, Sligo,

And full-right Antrim —

A kiss of your mouth,

Sure it were dearer to myself

  Than all that put together and let me get it.

Translated by Douglas Hyde

Portrait of a Lady
Nathaniel Hone (1718–1784)

from THE MIDNIGHT COURT
Brian Merriman

Then up there jumps from a neighbouring chair
A little old man with a spiteful air,
Staggering legs and panting breath,
And a look in his eye like poison and death;
And this apparition stumps up the hall
And says to the girl in the hearing of all:
'Damnation take you, you bastard's bitch,
Got by a tinkerman under a ditch!
No wonder the seasons are all upsot,
Nor every beating Ireland got;
Decline in decency and manners,
And the cows gone dry and the price of bonhams!
Mavrone! what more can we expect
With Doll and Moll and the way they're decked?
You slut of ill-fame, allow your betters
To tell the court how you learned your letters!
Your seed and breed for all your brag
Were tramps to a man with rag and bag;
I knew your da and what passed for his wife,
And he shouldered his traps to the end of his life,
An aimless lout without friend or neighbour,
Knowledge or niceness, wit or favour:
The breeches he wore were riddled with holes
And his boots without a tack of the soles.
Believe me, friends, if you sold at a fair,

Himself and his wife, his kids and gear,
When the costs were met, by the Holy Martyr,
You'd still go short for a glass of porter.
But the devil's child has the devil's cheek —
You that never owned cow nor sheep,
With buckles and brogues and rings to order —
You that were reared in the reek of solder!
However the rest of the world is gypped
I knew you when you went half-stripped;
And I'd venture a guess that in what you lack
A shift would still astonish your back;
And, shy as you seem, an inquisitive gent
Might study the same with your full consent.
Bosom and back are tightly laced,
Or is it the stays that gives you the waist?
Oh, all can see the way you shine,
But your looks are no concern of mine.
Now tell us the truth and don't be shy
How long are you eating your dinner dry?
A meal of spuds without butter or milk,
And dirt in layers beneath the silk.
Bragging and gab are yours by right,
But I know too where you sleep at night,
And blanket or quilt you never saw
But a strip of old mat and a bundle of straw,

In a hovel of mud without a seat,
And slime that settles about your feet,
A carpet of weeds from door to wall
And hens inscribing their tracks on all;
The rafters in with a broken back
And brown rain lashing through every crack —
'Twas there you learned to look so nice,
But now may we ask how you came by the price?
We all admired the way you spoke,
But whisper, treasure, who paid for the cloak?
A sparrow with you would die of hunger —
How did you come by all the grandeur,
All the tassels and all the lace —
Would you have us believe they were got in grace?
The frock made a hole in somebody's pocket,
And it wasn't you that paid for the jacket;
But assuming that and the rest no news,
How the hell did you come by the shoes?

'Your worship, 'tis women's sinful pride
And that alone has the world destroyed.
Every young man that's ripe for marriage
Is hooked like this by some tricky baggage,
And no one is secure, for a friend of my own,
As nice a boy as ever I've known
That lives from me only a perch or two —

God help him! — married misfortune too.
It breaks my heart when she passes by
With her saucy looks and head held high,
Cows to pasture and fields of wheat,
And money to spare — and all deceit!
Well-fitted to rear a tinker's clan,
She waggles her hips at every man,
With her brazen face and bullock's hide,
And such airs and graces, and mad with pride.
And — that God may judge me! — only I hate
A scandalous tongue, I could relate
Things of that woman's previous state
As one with whom every man could mate
In any convenient field or gate
As the chance might come to him early or late!
But now, of course, we must all forget
Her galloping days and the pace she set;
The race she ran in Ibrackane,
In Manishmore and Teermaclane,
With young and old of the meanest rabble
Of Ennis, Clareabbey and Quin astraddle!
Toughs from Tradree out on a fling,
And Cratlee cutthroats sure to swing;
But still I'd say 'twas the neighbours' spite,
And the girl did nothing but what was right,

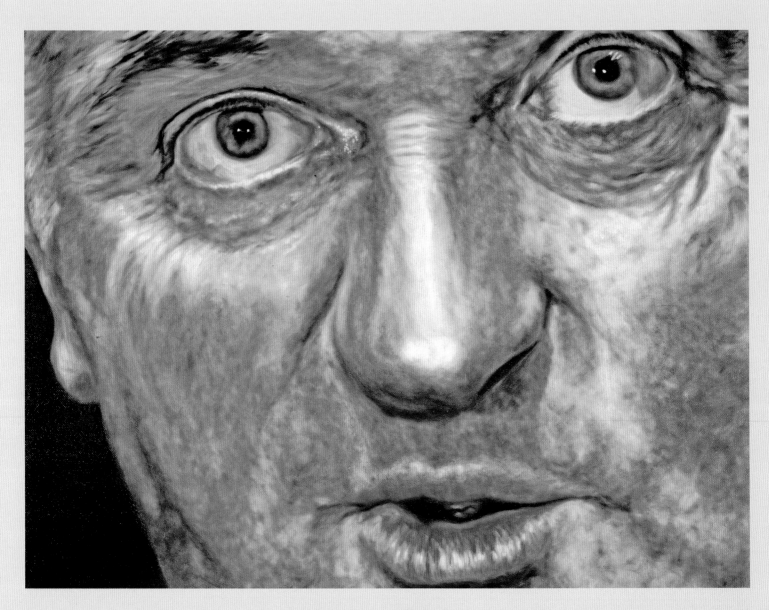

Fish Eyed (2009)
Dermot Seymour (1956–)

But the devil take her and all she showed!
I found her myself on the public road,
On the naked earth with a bare backside
And a Garus turf-cutter astride!
Is it any wonder my heart is failing,
That I feel that the end of the world is nearing,
When, ploughed and sown to all men's knowledge,
She can manage the child to arrive with marriage,
And even then, put to the pinch,
Begrudges Charity an inch;
For, counting from the final prayer
With the candles quenched and the altar bare
To the day when her offspring takes the air
Is a full nine months with a week to spare?

'But you see the troubles a man takes on!
From the minute he marries his peace is gone;
Forever in fear of a neighbour's sneer —
And my own experience cost me dear.
I lived alone as happy as Larry
Till I took it into my head to marry,
Tilling my fields with an easy mind,
Going wherever I felt inclined,
Welcomed by all as a man of price,
Always ready with good advice.

The neighbours listened — they couldn't refuse
For I'd money and stock to uphold my views —
Everything came at my beck and call
Till a woman appeared and destroyed it all:
A beautiful girl with ripening bosom,
Cheeks as bright as apple-blossom,
Hair that glimmered and foamed in the wind,
And a face that blazed with the light behind;
A tinkling laugh and a modest carriage
And a twinkling eye that was ripe for marriage.
I goggled and gaped like one born mindless
Till I took her face for a form of kindness,
Though that wasn't quite what the Lord intended
For He marked me down like a man offended
For a vengeance that wouldn't be easy mended
With my folly exposed and my comfort ended.

'Not to detain you here all day
I married the girl without more delay,
And took my share in the fun that followed.
There was plenty for all and nothing borrowed.
Be fair to me now! There was no one slighted;
The beggarmen took the road delighted;
The clerk and mummers were elated;
The priest went home with his pocket weighted.

The lamps were lit, the guests arrived;
The supper was ready, the drink was plied;
The fiddles were flayed, and, the night advancing,
The neighbours joined in the sport and dancing.

'A pity to God I didn't smother
When first I took the milk from my mother,
Or any day I ever broke bread
Before I brought that woman to bed!
For though everyone talked of her carouses
As a scratching post of the publichouses
That as sure as ever the glasses would jingle
Flattened herself to married and single,
Admitting no modesty to mention,
I never believed but 'twas all invention.
They added, in view of the life she led,
I might take to the roads and beg my bread,
But I took it for talk and hardly minded —
Sure, a man like me could never be blinded! —
And I smiled and nodded and off I tripped
Till my wedding night when I saw her stripped,
And knew too late that this was no libel
Spread in the pub by some jealous rival —
By God, 'twas a fact, and well-supported:
I was a father before I started!

'So there I was in the cold daylight,
A family man after one short night!
The women around me, scolding, preaching,
The wife in bed and the baby screeching.
I stirred the milk as the kettle boiled
Making a bottle to give the child;
All the old hags at the hob were cooing
As if they believed it was all my doing —
Flattery worse than ever you heard:
"Glory and praise to our blessed Lord,
Though he came in a hurry, the poor little creature,
He's the spit of his da in every feature.
Sal, will you look at the cut of that lip!
There's fingers for you! Feel his grip!
Would you measure the legs and the rolls of fat!
Was there ever a seven month child like that?"
And they traced away with great preciseness
My matchless face in the baby's likeness;
The same snub nose and frolicsome air,
And the way I laugh and the way I stare;
And they swore that never from head to toe
Was a child that resembled his father so.
But they wouldn't let me go near the wonder —
"Sure, a draught would blow the poor child
asunder!"

All of them out to blind me further —
"The least little breath would be noonday murder!"
Malice and lies! So I took the floor,
Mad with rage and I cursed and swore,
And bade them all to leave my sight.
They shrank away with faces white,
And moaned as they handed me the baby:
"Don't crush him now! Can't you handle him easy?
The least thing hurts them. Treat him kindly!
Some fall she got brought it on untimely.
Don't lift his head but leave him lying!
Poor innocent scrap, and to think he's dying!
If he lives at all till the end of day
Till the priest can come 'tis the most we'll pray!"

'I off with the rags and set him free,
And studied him well as he lay on my knee.
That too, by God, was nothing but lies
For he staggered myself with his kicks and cries.
A pair of shoulders like my own,
Legs like sausages, hair fullgrown;
His ears stuck out and his nails were long,
His hands and wrists and elbows strong;
His eyes were bright, his nostrils wide,
And the knee-caps showing beneath his hide —
A champion, begod, a powerful whelp,
As healthy and hearty as myself!

Translated by Frank O'Connor

To —

Thomas Moore

When I loved you, I can't but allow
I had many an exquisite minute;
But the scorn that I feel for you now
Hath even more luxury in it!

Thus, whether we're on or we're off,
Some witchery seems to await you;
To love you is pleasant enough
And oh! 'tis delicious to hate you!

*Queens Who Wasted the East
by Proxy (1914)*
Harry Clarke (1889–1931)

SHULE AROON

Anon (18th century)

I would I were on yonder hill,
'Tis there I'd sit and cry my fill,
And every tear would turn a mill,
Is go d-teidh tu, a mhiúrnín slán!

 Siubhail, siubhail, siubhail, a rúin!
 Siubhail go socair, agus siubhail go ciúin;
 Siubhail go d-ti an doras agus eulaigh liom,
 Is go d-teidh tu, a mhiúrnín slán!★

I'll sell my rock, I'll sell my reel,
I'll sell my only spinning-wheel,
To buy for my love a sword of steel,
Is go d-teidh tu, a mhiúrnín slán!

 Siubhail, siubhail, siubhail, a rúin!
 Siubhail go socair, agus siubhail go ciúin;
 Siubhail go d-ti an doras agus eulaigh liom,
 Is go d-teidh tu, a mhiúrnín slán!

I'll dye my petticoats, I'll dye them red,
And round the world I'll beg my bread,
Until my parents shall wish me dead,
Is go d-teidh tu, a mhiúrnín slán!

 Siubhail, siubhail, siubhail, a rúin!
 Siubhail go socair, agus siubhail go ciúin;
 Siubhail go d-ti an doras agus eulaigh liom,
 Is go d-teidh tu, a mhiúrnín slán!

I wish, I wish, I wish in vain,
I wish I had my heart again,
And vainly think I'd not complain,
Is go d-teidh tu, a mhiúrnín slán!

 Siubhail, siubhail, siubhail, a rúin!
 Siubhail go socair, agus siubhail go ciúin;
 Siubhail go d-ti an doras agus eulaigh liom,
 Is go d-teidh tu, a mhiúrnín slán!

But now my love has gone to France,
To try his fortune to advance;
If he e'er come back, 'tis but a chance,
Is go d-teidh tu, a mhiúrnín slán!

 Siubhail, siubhail, siubhail, a rúin!
 Siubhail go socair, agus siubhail go ciúin;
 Siubhail go d-ti an doras agus eulaigh liom,
 Is go d-teidh tu, a mhiúrnín slán!

Translated by George Sigerson

★ And safe for aye may my darling be!
  Come, come, come, O Love!
  Quickly come to me, softly move;
  Come to the door, and away we'll flee,
  And safe for aye may my darling be!

Landed Angel (2006)
Charles Harper (1943–)

Serenade (for Music)

Oscar Wilde

The western wind is blowing fair
    Across the dark Aegean sea,
And at the secret marble stair
    My Tyrian galley waits for thee.
Come down! the purple sail is spread,
    The watchman sleeps within the town,
O leave thy lily-flowered bed,
    O Lady mine come down, come down!

She will not come, I know her well,
    Of lover's vows she hath no care,
And little good a man can tell
    Of one so cruel and so fair.
True love is but a woman's toy,
    They never know the lover's pain,
And I who loved as loves a boy
    Must love in vain, must love in vain.

O noble pilot, tell me true,
    Is that the sheen of golden hair?
Or is it but the tangled dew
    That binds the passion-flowers there?
Good sailor come and tell me now
    Is that my Lady's lily hand?
Or is it but the gleaming prow,
    Or is it but the silver sand?

No! no! 'tis not the tangled dew,
    'Tis not the silver-fretted sand,
It is my own dear Lady true
    With golden hair and lily hand!
O noble pilot, steer for Troy,
    Good sailor, ply the labouring oar,
This is the Queen of life and joy
    Whom we must bear from Grecian shore!

The waning sky grows faint and blue,
    It wants an hour still of day,
Aboard! aboard! my gallant crew,
    O Lady mine; away! away!
O noble pilot, steer for Troy,
    Good sailor, ply the labouring oar,
O loved as only loves a boy!
    O loved for ever evermore!

Lovers and Stars
Pauline Bewick (1935–)

TO THE BELOVED

Alice Furlong

Love of you and hate of you
Tears my very heart in two!
As you please me or displease,
So I burn and so I freeze.

I would build your wattled dun
With a gold roof like the sun;
I would stain the trellis bars
With the silver of the stars.

At my bitter heart's behoof
I would wreck your radiant roof;
Of your twinkling trellises
All my anger jealous is.

I would give you great-horned rams,
Mild-eyed sheep, and milk-white lambs,
Fit for any king to own,
By the turning of the stone.

I would set your rams astray,
I would wile your sheep away,
With their lambs' milk-white exceeding,
For the grey wolf's famished feeding.

I would guide the oxen meek,
And the ploughshare's silver beak
O'er your land to make it meet
For the sowing of the wheat.

I would blight your team with blain,
I would rust your ploughs with rain,
In your furrows, deep and brown,
I would scatter thistle-down.

I would put twelve milking cows
On your pastures green to browse;
I would set twelve tubs of cream
On your dairy's oaken beam.

Blasted by a curse of mine,
All your cows should ail and pine;
From your fields I'd skim the dew —
Steal the cream away from you.

Under your grey apple trees
I would hive the honey bees;
Store away in each gold dome
Lush, delicious honey-comb.

From the boughs of rose and grey
I would charm the bees away,
Bitter bread might be your share
On the days of Easter fare.

I would crown your head with gold,
Robe you fine in silken fold,
Win for you a magic wand
From Danaan fairy-land.

I would break your golden crown,
I would rend your silken gown,
I would burn your magic wand
From Danaan fairy-land.

I would place you on a throne,
I would give you all to own,
All of me and all of mine:
I would make you half-divine.

I would leave you in sore want,
I would have you hunger-gaunt,
I would bring you to my feet
In subjection most complete.

I would lift you to the skies,
I would give you paradise;
I would suffer hell's worst dole
For the saving of your soul.

Wounding coldness to reprove
I would wound you in my love.
Suppliant still at your heart's gate
I do worship in my hate.

The Piper
Grace Henry (1868–1953)

ENTREATY
Caitlín Maude

Young man,

do not come near me,

do not speak ...

the words of love

are sweet —

but sweeter still

is the word

that was never uttered —

no choice

is without stain —

the choice of words

is much the same

and this would be

to choose between

evils in our present

situation ...

Do not break

the clear glass

between us

   (no glass is broken

    without blood and pain)

for beyond is

Heaven

or beyond is Hell

and what good is

Heaven

if it is not

for ever? —

the loss of

Heaven

is the worst Hell ...

I again implore you,

do not speak,

young man,

my 'Diarmaid',

and we will be at peace —

untouchable understanding

between us

we will have no cause

to touch it

ever

as it ever

alures us —

but I implore you ...

do not speak ...

Translated by Gabriel Fitzmaurice

Anna Maria Ferri (c.1790–92)
Robert Fagan (c.1745–1816)

Composition with Figures (1936)
Mainie Jellett (1897–1944)

DEAD LOVES

Reverie (1914)
Anne Marjorie Robinson (1858–1924)

Sad is his voice that calls me, sadly calling

On the Death of His Wife

Muireadhach Albanach Ó Dálaigh

I parted from my life last night,
   A woman's body sunk in clay:
The tender bosom that I loved
   Wrapped in a sheet they took away.

The heavy blossom that had lit
   The ancient boughs is tossed and blown;
Hers was the burden of delight
   That long had weighed the old tree down.

And I am left alone tonight
   And desolate is the world I see,
For lovely was that woman's weight
   That even last night had lain on me.

Weeping I look upon the place
   Where she used to rest her head —
For yesterday her body's length
   Reposed upon you too, my bed.

Yesterday that smiling face
   Upon one side of you was laid
That could match the hazel bloom
   In its dark delicate sweet shade.

Maelva of the shadowy brows
   was the mead-cask at my side;
Fairest of all flowers that grow
   Was the beauty that has died.

My body's self deserts me now,
   The half of me that was her own,
Since all I knew of brightness died
   Half of me lingers, half is gone.

The face that was like hawthorn bloom
   Was my right foot and my right side;
And my right hand and my right eye
   Were no more mine than hers who died.

Poor is the share of me that's left
 Since half of me died with my wife;
I shudder at the words I speak;
 Dear God, that girl was half my life.

And our first look was her first love;
 No man had fondled ere I came
The little breasts so small and firm
 And the long body like a flame.

For twenty years we shared a home,
 Our converse milder with each year;
Eleven children in its time
 Did that tall stately body bear.

It was the King of hosts and roads
 Who snatched her from me in her prime:
Little she wished to leave alone
 The man she loved before her time.

Now King of churches and of bells,
 Though never raised to pledge a lie
That woman's hand — can it be true? —
 No more beneath my head will lie.

Translated by Frank O'Connor

Self Portrait in Suburban Garden, 1965
Brian Bourke (1936–)

I AM STRETCHED ON YOUR GRAVE

Anon (18th century)

I am stretched on your grave
   And would lie there forever;
If your hands were in mine
   I'd be sure we'd not sever.
My apple tree, my brightness,
   'Tis time we were together
For I smell of the earth
   And am stained by the weather.

When my family thinks
   That I'm safe in my bed
From night until morning
   I am stretched at your head,
Calling out to the air
   With tears hot and wild
My grief for the girl
   That I loved as a child.

Do you remember
   The night we were lost
In the shade of the blackthorn
   And the chill of the frost?
Thanks be to Jesus
   We did what was right,
And your maidenhead still
   Is your pillar of light.

The priests and the friars
   Approach me in dread
Because I still love you
   My love and you dead,
And would still be your shelter
   From rain and from storm,
And with you in the cold grave
   I cannot sleep warm.

Translated by Frank O'Connor

Evening Shoreline, Mayo, 2001
Mary Lohan (1954–)

THE LAMENT FOR ART O'LEARY
Eileen O'Connell

My love and my delight,
The day I saw you first
Beside the markethouse
I had eyes for nothing else
And love for none but you.

I left my father's house
And ran away with you,
And that was no bad choice;
You gave me everything.
There were parlours whitened for me,
Bedrooms painted for me,
Ovens reddened for me,
Loaves baked for me,
Joints spitted for me,
Beds made for me
To take my ease on flock
Until the milking time
And later if I pleased.

My mind remembers
That bright spring day,
How your hat with its band
Of gold became you,
Your silver-hilted sword,
Your manly right hand,
Your horse on her mettle
And foes around you
Cowed by your air;
For when you rode by
On your white-nosed mare
The English lowered their head before you
Not out of love for you
But hate and fear.
For, sweetheart of my soul,
The English killed you.

My love and my calf
Of the race of the Earls of Antrim
And the Barrys of Eemokilly,
How well a sword became you,
A hat with a band,
A slender foreign shoe
And a suit of yarn
Woven over the water!

My love and my darling
When I go home
The little lad, Conor,
And Fiach the baby
Will surely ask me
Where I left their father,
I'll say with anguish
'Twas in Kilnamartyr;
They will call the father
Who will never answer.

My love and my mate
That I never thought dead
Till your horse came to me
With bridle trailing,
All blood from forehead
To polished saddle
Where you should be,
Either sitting or standing;
I gave one leap to the threshold,
A second to the gate,
A third upon its back.

I clapped my hands,
And off at a gallop;
I never lingered
Till I found you lying
By a little furze-bush
Without pope or bishop
Or priest or cleric
One prayer to whisper
But an old, old woman,
And her cloak about you,
And your blood in torrents —
Art O'Leary —
I did not wipe it off,
I drank it from my palms.

My love and my delight
Stand up now beside me,
And let me lead you home
Until I make a feast,
And I will roast the meat
And send for company
And call the harpers in,
And I shall make your bed
Of soft and snowy sheets
And blankets dark and rough
To warm the beloved limbs
An autumn blast has chilled.

(His sister speaks)

My little love, my calf,
This is the image
That last night brought me
In Cork all lonely
On my bed sleeping,
That the white courtyard
And the tall mansion
That we two played in
As children had fallen,
Ballingeary withered
And your hounds were silent,
Yours birds were songless
While people found you
On the open mountain
Without priest or cleric
But an old, old woman
And her coat about you
When the earth caught you —
Art O'Leary —
And your life-blood stiffened
The white shirt on you.

My love and treasure,
Where is the woman
From Cork of the white sails
To the bridge of Tomey
With her dowry gathered
And cows at pasture
Would sleep alone
The night they waked you?

(His wife replies)

My darling, do not believe
One word she is saying,
It is a falsehood
That I slept while others
Sat up to wake you —
'Twas no sleep that took me
But the children crying;
They would not rest
Without me beside them.

The Widow (1882)
Frank O'Meara (1853–1888)

O people, do not believe
Any lying story!
There is no woman in Ireland
Who had slept beside him
And borne him three children
But would cry out
After Art O'Leary
Who lies dead before me
Since yesterday morning.

Grief on you, Morris!
Heart's blood and bowels' blood!
May your eyes go blind
And your knees be broken!
You killed my darling
And no man in Ireland
Will fire the shot at you.

Destruction pursue you,
Morris the traitor
Who brought death to my husband!
Father of three children —
Two on the hearth
And one in the womb
That I shall not bring forth.

It is my sorrow
That I was not by
When they fired the shots
To catch them in my dress
Or in my heart, who cares?
If you but reached the hills
Rider of the ready hands.

My love and my fortune
'Tis an evil portion
To lay for a giant —
A shroud and a coffin —
For a big-hearted hero
Who fished in the hill-streams
And drank in bright halls
With white-breasted women.

My comfort and my friend,
Master of the bright sword,
'Tis time you left your sleep;
Yonder hangs your whip,
Your horse is at the door,
Follow the lane to the east
Where every bush will bend
And every stream dry up,
And man and woman bow
If things have manners yet
That have them not I fear.

Esmerelda (1942)
Colin Middleton (1910–1983)

My love and my sweetness,
'Tis not the death of my people,
Donal Mor O'Connell,
Connell who died by drowning,
Or the girl of six and twenty
Who went across the water
To be a queen's companion —
'Tis not all these I speak of
And call in accents broken
But noble Art O'Leary,
Art of hair so golden,
Art of wit and courage,
Art the brown mare's master,
Swept last night to nothing
Here in Carriganimma —
Perish it, name and people!

My love and my treasure,
Though I bring with me
No throng of mourners,
'Tis no shame for me,
For my kinsmen are wrapped in
A sleep beyond waking,
In narrow coffins
Walled up in stone.

Though but for the smallpox,
And the black death,
And the spotted fever,
That host of riders
With bridles shaking
Would wake the echoes,
Coming to your waking,
Art of the white breast.

Could my calls but wake my kindred
In Derrynane beyond the mountains,
Or Capling of the yellow apples,
Many a proud and stately rider,
Many a girl with spotless kerchief,
Would be here before tomorrow,
Shedding tears about your body,
Art O'Leary, once so merry.

Lord Newbottle (1762)
Robert Hunter (*c.*1720–1803)

My love and my secret,
Your corn is stacked,
Your cows are milking;
On me is the grief
There's no cure for in Munster.
Till Art O'Leary rise
This grief will never yield
That's bruising all my heart
Yet shut up fast in it,
As 'twere in a locked trunk
With the key gone astray,
And rust grown on the wards.

My love and my calf,
Noble Art O'Leary,
Son of Conor, son of Cady,
Son of Lewis O'Leary,
West of the Valley
And east of Greenane
Where berries grow thickly
And nuts crowd on branches
And apples in heaps fall
In their own season;
What wonder to any
If Iveleary lighted
And Ballingeary

And Gougane of the saints
For the smooth-palmed rider,
The unwearying huntsman
That I would see spurring
From Grenagh without halting
When quick hounds had faltered?
My rider of the bright eyes,
What happened you yesterday?
I thought you in my heart,
When I bought you your fine clothes,
A man the world could not slay.

'Tis known to Jesus Christ
Nor cap upon my head,
Nor shift upon my back,
Nor shoe upon my foot,
Nor gear in all my house,
Nor bridle for the mare
But I will spend at law;
And I'll go oversea
To plead before the King,
And if the King be deaf
I'll settle things alone
With the black-blooded rogue
That killed my man on me.

Rider of the white palms,
Go in to Baldwin,
And face the schemer,
The bandy-legged monster —
God rot him and his children!
(Wishing no harm to Maire,
Yet of no love for her,
But that my mother's body
Was a bed to her for three seasons
And to me beside her.)

Take my heart's love,
Dark women of the Mill,
For the sharp rhymes ye shed
On the rider of the brown mare.

But cease your weeping now,
Women of the soft, wet eyes
Till Art O'Leary drink
Ere he go to the dark school —
Not to learn music or song
But to prop the earth and the stone.

Translated by Frank O'Connor

A QUESTION

J.M. Synge

I asked if I got sick and died; would you
With my black funeral go walking too,
If you'd stand close to hear them talk or pray
While I'm let down in that steep bank of clay.

And, No, you said, for if you saw a crew
Of living idiots, pressing round that new
Oak coffin — they alive, I dead beneath
That board — you'd rave and rend them with your teeth.

While Grass Grows (1936)
Jack B. Yeats (1871–1957)

SHE WEEPS OVER RAHOON

James Joyce

Rain on Rahoon falls softly, softly falling,
Where my dark lover lies.
Sad is his voice that calls me, sadly calling,
At grey moonrise.

Love, hear thou
How soft, how sad his voice is ever calling,
Ever unanswered, and the dark rain falling,
Then as now.

Dark too our hearts, O love, shall lie and cold
As his sad heart has lain
Under the moongrey nettles, the black mould
And muttering rain.

Pensive Woman in Grey (1895)
Sarah Purser (1848–1943)

LUST

Nick Laird

the one   who went on to become   Mrs Laird

the wife   walked into my life

one night   I'd had six or seven pints

and it was either that or fight

and she was just the type   I like

chest spilling out of itself   slender-hipped

with a Nubian face closed to the public

waist   my exact hand-span

poised and filmic   she was drinking my usual

unthinkable and very

very do-able   I am not a good man

into my grave into my grave into my grave she was laid

Girl With a Tongue of Water Cried (1961)
Jack Pakenham (1938–)

Poets' Biographies

George Buchanan (1904–1989), a poet and novelist, was born in Co. Antrim and educated in Belfast. After a move to England he worked in journalism. His perceptive novels are concerned with the trials of middle-class life and, in particular, the situation of women: *The Soldier and the Girl* (1940) and *A Place to Live* (1952). *The Green Seacoast* (1959) is an autobiography set during the political turmoil of his youth in Ireland. Poetry collections include *Conversation with Strangers* (1959) and *Inside Traffic* (1976).

Jeremiah Joseph Callanan (1795–1829), a poet and folklorist, was born in Co. Cork and educated at Maynooth seminary and Trinity College Dublin. His poetry in English is strongly influenced by the metrics and verse forms of writing in Irish. As a folklorist and song collector he travelled widely throughout the south of Ireland. The majority of his work, including the long Byronic poem *The Recluse of Inchydoney* (1830), was published posthumously.

Séathrún Céitinn/Geoffrey Keating (*c*.1580–*c*.1644), a theologian and historian, was born in Co. Tipperary and educated for the priesthood in France, at Reims and Bordeaux. In Ireland he worked as a preacher and theological writer. His most significant literary work, *Foras Feasa ar Éirinn* (1634), a history of Ireland from earliest times to the Anglo Norman invasion of the twelfth century, had a profound influence on subsequent Irish historical writing and earned him the title of 'the Herodotus of Ireland'. His poetry is known for its beauty of language in the original Irish.

E.R. Dodds (1893–1979), an academic and poet, was born in Belfast and educated at Oxford where he subsequently held the Chair of Greek (1936–1960). He was also President of the Society for Psychical Research (1961–1963). His many publications include *Select Passages Illustrating Neoplatonism* (1923) and *The Ancient Concept of Progress and other Essays on Greek Literature and Belief* (1973). He published an autobiography, *Missing Persons* (1979).

James Doherty (attrib., dates unknown). The witty love song 'I'd swear for her' is attributed to Doherty of whom, otherwise, nothing is known. The ironic tone and lyric form of the composition suggest a late nineteenth-century date, while the Lough Erne reference locating the poem to Co. Fermanagh may confirm that the writer was resident in that area.

Katie Donovan (1962–), a poet and academic, was born in Co. Leitrim. She studied at Trinity College Dublin and the University of California. She has worked as a journalist and critic. Her poetry combines intensity and intimacy in vignettes of domestic life. Her collections are *Watermelon Man* (1993), *Entering the Mare* (1997), *Day of the Dead* (2002) and, most recently, *Rootling: New and Selected Poems* (2010).

Seán Dunne (1956–1995), a poet and broadcaster, was born in Co. Waterford and educated at University College Cork. His collections include *Against the Storm* (1985) and *The Sheltered Nest* (1992). He published a sensitive memoir, *In My Father's House* (1991), was editor of *Poets of Munster* (1995) and compiler of *The Cork Anthology* (1993).

Paul Durcan (1944–), a poet, was born in Dublin and educated at University College Cork. A noted social satirist, his distinct poetic voice has established him as a significant commentator on public and private life: *A Snail in My Prime*: *New and Selected Poems* (1993), and *Greetings to our Friends in Brazil* (1999). Two singular collections, *Crazy about Women* (1991) and *Give me Your Hand* (1994), are based on the art collections of, respectively, the National Galleries of Dublin and London. *Life is a Dream: 40 Years of Reading Poems 1967–2008* (2009) is a selection from his lifetime's work.

Alice Furlong (1875–1946), a poet and political activist, was born in Co. Dublin. She was a founder member of *Inghinidhe na hÉireann* (Daughters of Ireland) and opposed the 1900 visit of Queen Victoria to Dublin. Among her publications are *Rose and Rues* (1899) and *Tales of Fairy Folk* (1907).

Patrick Galvin (1927–2011), a poet, playwright and memoirist, was born in Cork. Galvin wrote a number of volumes of acclaimed autobiography, including *Song* *of a Poor Boy* (1989) and *Song for a Raggy Boy* (1991). He is noted in particular for his poem 'The Mad Woman of Cork'. His work is strongly influenced by urban folklore and the ballad tradition. Between 1974 and 1978 he was playwright in residence at the Lyric Theatre, Belfast.

Gerald Griffin (1803–1840), a playwright, novelist and poet, was born in Limerick but emigrated to London to pursue a career as a journalist. *Holland-Tide* (1826), a collection of stories, and a novel, *The Collegians* (1829), are among his more successful literary works. The latter became the basis for Dion Boucicault's play *The Colleen Bawn* (1860) and an opera *The Lilly of Killarney* (1862) by Sir Julius Benedict. Griffin abandoned writing in 1838, burnt his manuscripts and entered the Christian Brothers, a religious teaching order.

Vona Groarke (1964–), a poet and academic, was born in Co. Longford and educated at Trinity College Dublin and Cork University. A multi-award-winning poet, she represents a significant advance in contemporary women's poetry. Her collections are *Shale* (1994), *Other People's Houses* (1999) and *Flight* (2002). Her most recent collection is *Spindrift* (2009).

Seamus Heaney (1939–2013), a poet, essayist and critic, was born in Co. Derry and educated at Queen's University, Belfast, where he later taught. He subsequently became Professor of Rhetoric at Harvard University and Professor of Poetry at Oxford, and was the 1995 recipient of the Noble Prize for Literature. He was the most celebrated of contemporary Irish poets. His works include *Death of a Naturalist* (1966), *North* (1975), *The Haw Lantern* (1987), versions of plays from Sophocles, and translations, including the Anglo Saxon *Beowulf* (1999). His final collection was *Human Chain* (2010).

Esther Johnson/'Stella' (1681–1728), muse and bluestocking, grew up at Moore Park, Surrey, home of the diplomat Sir William Temple where Jonathan Swift, working as Temple's secretary, met her in 1689 and became her tutor. In 1701 she moved to Dublin to be near Swift but the nature of their relationship is ambiguous. From 1719 he wrote annual 'Birthday Poems' to her. She is buried next to Swift in St Patrick's Cathedral, Dublin, where he was Dean.

James Joyce (1882–1941), a writer, was born in Dublin and educated at the Royal University, Dublin. He left Ireland in 1904 and lived for the rest of his life in various Continental countries, finally settling in Paris. One of the leading experimental writers of the twentieth century, his early work includes a volume of short stories, *Dubliners* (1914), and *A Portrait of the Artist as a Young Man* (1916). Two major novels followed, *Ulysses* (1922) and *Finnegans Wake* (1939), both landmarks in modern writing. His two volumes of poetry are *Chamber Music* (1907) and *Poems Pennyeach* (1927).

Patrick Kavanagh (1904–1967), a poet and novelist, was born in Inniskeen, Co. Monaghan to a farming family on a nine-acre holding. He was self-educated and read extensively. He began writing verse at a young age and submitted poems to local and national newspapers. His major prose works are *The Green Fool* (1938) and *Tarry Flynn* (1948). His poetry includes the long poem *The Great Hunger* (1942), his greatest achievement, and *Come Dance with Kitty Stobling* (1960). Kavanagh is the most significant Irish twentieth-century poet alongside W.B. Yeats and Seamus Heaney. In the introduction to *Collected Poems* (1964), Kavanagh wrote, 'A man innocently dabbles in words and rhymes and finds that it is his life'.

Thomas Kinsella (1928–), a poet, was born in Inchicore, Dublin, and was educated at University College Dublin. A poet, anthologist and translator, and a major figure in Irish writing, he spent many years as an academic in the United States. His collections include *Nightwalker and Other Poems* (1968), *Notes from the Land of the Dead* (1972), *Fifteen Dead* (1976) and *Thomas Kinsella: Collected Poems* (1956–2001). *The Tain* (1969) and *An Duanaire, 1600–1900: Poems of the Dispossessed* with Seán Ó Tuama (1981) are landmark translations.

Nick Laird (1975–), a poet and novelist, was born in Co. Tyrone. He studied at Cambridge and was a visiting fellow at Harvard University. Poetry publications include *To a Fault* (2005), *On Purpose* (2007), *Go Giants* (2013), and novels *Utterly Monkey* (2005) and *Glover's Mistake* (2009). He has won many awards for his writing, including the Eric Gregory Award (2004), the Rooney Prize for Irish Literature (2005), the Somerset Maugham Award and the Geoffery Faber Memorial Prize (2007).

Patrick MacDonogh (1902–1961), a poet and athlete, was born in Co. Dublin and educated at Trinity College Dublin. He published six volumes of poetry between 1929 and 1958. His poetry ranges from exquisite love lyrics to verse concerned with the moral failures of the emergent Irish Republic of his time. Collections include *Flirtation* (1927), *A Leaf in the Wind* (1929) and *Over the Water and Other Poems* (1943).

Medbh McGuckian (1950–), a poet, anthologist and teacher, was born in Belfast, educated at Queen's University, Belfast, and a visiting fellow at the University of Berkeley. Her publications made a significant contribution to women's writing and include *On Ballycastle Beach* (1988), *Marconi's Cottage* (1991) and *The Lavender Hat* (1994).

Louis MacNeice (1907–1963), a poet, was born in Belfast and educated at the University of Oxford. Also a playwright and critic, he worked for twenty years as a literary producer at the BBC. His extensive output places him as the major writer of his time from Northern Ireland. *The Collected Poems of Louis MacNeice* (1966) was edited by E.R. Dodds (see above).

Derek Mahon (1942–) was born in Belfast and educated at Trinity College Dublin. A poet and literary journalist, he is noted for his command of the long poem and lyric poetry. Amongst his volumes of poetry are: *Poems 1962–1978* (1979), *The Hudson Letter* (1995), *The Yellow Book* (1997) and *Collected Poems* (1999). He has also translated works from French, including Edmond Rostand's *Cyrano de Bergerac*.

Caitlín Maude (1941–1982) was born in Co. Galway and educated at University College Galway. Poet, academic, actress, broadcaster and *sean-nós* singer, she was a polemicist for the Irish language and for civil rights. Publications include *An Lasair Choille* (with Michael Hartnett, 1961) and her collected poems, *Danta* (1984).

Brian Merriman (?1745–1805) was born in Ennistimon, Co. Clare. He was a farmer and teacher, and is particularly remembered for his long (1,026-line) poem in Irish, *Cúirt an Mheán-Oíche*/*The Midnight Court* (1780), a satire on contemporary sexuality and marriage, which, together with other Gaelic satires, had an influence on the modern-day writings of Seamus Heaney and Thomas Kinsella.

John Montague (1929–), born in New York, was educated at University College Dublin. He is a poet, prose writer and academic, and the first holder of the Ireland Chair of Poetry (1998). A noted commentator on both personal and public issues, he has published widely: *The Rough Field* (1972),

The Great Cloak (1978), *An Occasion of Sin* (1992) and *Collected Poems* (1995).

Thomas Moore (1779–1852), a poet, singer, songwriter and entertainer, was born in Dublin and educated at Trinity College Dublin. He is best remembered for his 'Irish Melodies' (1808–1834), which popularised Irish culture with Victorian audiences. Many of his lyrics set to traditional Irish airs have retained their popularity. He was responsible, with the publisher John Murray, for burning Lord Byron's memoirs after the poet's death.

Úna Ní Bhroin (d. *c*.1706), a poet, was probably born in Co. Roscommon. She was related to Edmund Byrne, Archbishop of Dublin (1707–1923). Scholars assumed that she received a good formal education. In *c*.1670 she married the writer Seán Ó Neachtain (see p.175) and moved with him to Dublin. Only a single poem by her has so far been identified.

Eibhlín Dubh Ní Chonaill/Eileen O'Connell (*c*.1745– *c*.1800) was a member of 'the Liberator', Daniel O'Connell's landed family, and was born at Derrynane, the O'Connell Kerry estate. Her second husband, Art Ó Laoghaire, a flamboyant captain in the Hungarian Hussars, was murdered in a dispute with the High Sheriff of Cork over possession of a horse. Scholars dispute whether the 'Lament for Art O'Leary' was actually written by his widow, Ní Chonaill, or is an outstanding example of a traditional literary form, composed collectively. It is, nonetheless, one of the great love poems of the nineteenth century.

Nuala Ní Dhomhnaill (1952–) was born in Lancashire and spent her childhood in the Gaeltacht, or Irish-speaking area of Dingle in Co. Kerry. She was educated at University College Cork. Apart from her poetry collections, her works include children's plays, screenplays, anthologies, articles, reviews and essays. One of the most well-known Irish-language poets, her poems appear in English translation in the dual-language editions *Selected Poems* (1986) and *The Astrakhan Coat* (1992).

Toirdhealbhach Ó Cearbhalláin/ Turlough O'Carolan (1670–1738), a musician, composer and poet, was born in Co. Meath. An attack of smallpox left him blind, but he trained as a harpist and became one of the most celebrated musicians of the period, influenced by both the native musical tradition and European Baroque compositions. Many of his tunes and poems are dedicated to young women or to his aristocratic patrons.

Muireadhach Albanach Ó Dálaigh (13th century), a poet, was born in Co. Meath to an important bardic family. In 1213 he murdered a tax collector and fled to Scotland. He subsequently went on pilgrimage to Jerusalem from where he returned to Ireland. Only a small number of his poems survive, which include deeply personal verse as well as official praise poems written for his patrons.

John O'Keeffe (1747–1833), a playwright, was born in Dublin and first studied art before settling on a career as an actor and writer. He moved to London in 1777. He wrote over sixty plays, including *Tony Lumpkin in Town* (1778) and *Wild Oats* (1791), and was the most produced playwright in London in the last quarter of the eighteenth century. The essayist William Hazlitt described him as the 'English Molière'.

Seán Ó Neachtain (*c.*1650–1729), a scholar, was born in Co. Roscommon but lived mostly in Dublin where he became a school teacher. His poems and prose compositions range widely from love poems to elegies and witty social commentary. His awareness of linguistic, ethnic and behavioural subtleties provided subject matter for a comic narrative *Cath Bearna Chroise Brighde*, and for poems satirising the clergy. He was married to Úna Ní Bhroin (see p.174).

John Boyle O'Reilly (1844–1890), a poet and political agitator, was born in Co. Louth. He worked as a journalist in Ireland and England, enlisting in the British Army in 1863 in order to recruit for the republican Fenian Brotherhood. He was sentenced to death in 1866 and, following a jailbreak, was transported to Australia. He escaped to America and became editor of the *Boston Pilot*, an influential Irish-American journal.

Eoghan Rua Ó Súilleabháin (1748–1784), a poet, was born in Co. Kerry. On account of the decline in Gaelic aristocratic patronage, he was forced to work as an itinerant labourer and schoolteacher, and later served in the British Navy under Admiral Rodney on the *Formidable*. Following a naval victory over the French fleet in 1782, he wrote *Rodney's Glory*. He wrote satires on contemporary figures and laments of great metrical skill in traditional *aisling* vision-poem mode. Editions of his poems began to be published from the early twentieth century.

Seán Ó Tuama (1926–2006), a poet, dramatist, critic and anthologist, was born in Cork and educated at University College Cork where he became Professor of Irish Language and Culture. His publications on contemporary Irish writing were highly influential, as were his editions of earlier Irish poetry: *Nuabhéarsaíocht* (1950), *An Gráin Amhráin na nDaoine* (1960), *An Duanaire, 1600–1900: Poems of the Dispossessed* (with Thomas Kinsella, 1981).

George 'AE' Russell (1867–1935), born in Lurgan, Co. Armagh, studied at the Metropolitan School of Art. He was a painter, poet, mystic, editor and agricultural co-operative organiser – a central figure of Irish cultural life – and his wide range of interests produced a distinguished body of work. He held a literary salon at his home in Rathmines.

James Simmons (1933–2001), a poet, literary critic and songwriter, was born in Derry, Northern Ireland. He attended

Campbell College in Belfast before moving to the University of Leeds to read English. In 1968 he accepted a teaching position at the recently-opened New University of Ulster in Coleraine, where he remained until his retirement in 1984. During the early 1970s he was the inspiration for The Resistance Cabaret, a satirical revue combining song, poetry and political comment on 'the troubles' and everyday life. He also took part in The Belfast Group, together with such writers as Michael Longley, Seamus Heaney and Derek Mahon. In 1968 he established *The Honest Ulsterman*, an important Irish literary journal, and served as the editor for 17 of the first 19 issues. Throughout his career Simmons wrote and performed exquisitely provocative, yet hilarious and humane, songs about every aspect of contemporary life. He recorded three collections of his own songs and produced a Resistance Cabaret album. He also set a number of Yeats' poems to music.

L.A.G. Strong (1896–1958), a novelist, poet and biographer, was born in Plymouth of Anglo Irish parents and was educated at Oxford University. He published six poetry collections, including a collected edition, *The Body's Imperfections* (1957), as well as many novels set in Ireland, in particular Dún Laoghaire where he spent his childhood holidays.

Jonathan Swift (1667–1745), a poet and satirist, was born in Dublin and educated at Trinity College. In 1697 he was ordained in the Church of Ireland, and later became Dean of St Patrick's Cathedral, Dublin.

Amongst the greatest satirists and political pamphleteers of his time, his major works are *Drapier's Letters* (1724–25), *Gulliver's Travels* (1726) and *A Modest Proposal* (1729). His love life and relationship with two women, Esther Johnson (Stella) and Esther Vanhomrigh (Vanessa) have been the source of endless speculation.

J.M. Synge (1871–1909), a playwright, was born in Dublin and educated at Trinity College. He was also a composer and poet and the author of a number of the most important plays of the Literary Revival. *The Shadow of the Glen* (1903) and *Riders to the Sea* (1904) were plays based on stories Synge had collected on the Aran Islands. *The Playboy of the Western World* (1907), widely regarded as his masterpiece, was first performed at Dublin's Abbey Theatre and attracted initial hostility from the Irish public.

Katharine Tynan (1861–1931), born in Co. Dublin, was a poet, novelist and journalist who played a major part in Dublin's literary circles. She was an important figure of the Literary Revival and a close associate of W.B. Yeats. Remarkably prolific, she published over 100 novels, five volumes of autobiography and her *Collected Poems* appeared in 1930.

Oscar Wilde (1856–1900) was born in Dublin and educated at Trinity College. A writer of enduring influence, he excelled as novelist, playwright and poet. *The Picture of Dorian Gray* (1889), *The Importance of Being Earnest* (1895), and *The Ballad of Reading*

Gaol (1898) are his major works. Convicted of homosexuality in 1895, he died in Paris shortly after his release from jail in England, aged forty-six.

Vincent Woods (1960–), a writer and broadcaster, was born in Co. Leitrim and educated at the College of Journalism, Dublin. His poetry collections are *The Colour of Language* (1994) and *Lives and Miracles* (2002). Well known as a playwright for provocative examinations of historical events, he has won numerous drama awards. Among his plays are *At the Black Pig's Dyke* (1992) and *Song of the Yellow Bittern* (1994).

Macdara Woods (1942–), a poet, was born in Dublin and educated at University College Dublin. He is one of the founders/editors of the literary journal *Cyphers*. He has worked as journalist and editor, and his extensive travels have produced a cosmopolitan body of work: *Selected Poems* (1996), *Knowledge in the Blood: New and Selected Poems* (2000), and *Collected Poems* (2012). His poems have been translated into many languages and set to music by distinguished composers.

W.B. Yeats (1865–1939), a poet and playwright, was born in Dublin and studied at the Metropolitan School of Art. One of the most influential poets of his age and a leading figure of the Literary Revival, he received the 1923 Nobel Prize for Literature. Yeats' spirituality and cultural nationalism became vehicles for some of the most memorable poetry in Irish literature.

Female Nude Study
Anonymous, Irish School, 20th century

ARTISTS' BIOGRAPHIES

Pauline Bewick (1935–) was born in Northumberland in northern England and moved to Ireland with her family in the late 1930s. In 1950 she went to the National College of Art in Dublin, and before long was commissioned to illustrate books and magazines; she also sang in a nightclub and became a set designer and actor with the Pike Theatre. She had her first exhibition in 1957 in the Clog Gallery, Dublin, and has since exhibited regularly in Ireland and in London. Her work has become very widely known for the freedom of her deeply sensuous draughtsmanship and for her qualities as a highly imaginative colourist.

Brian Bourke (1936–) was born in Dublin and studied at the National College of Art and Design in Dublin and St Martin's School of Art in London. In 1965 he represented Ireland at both the Paris Biennale and the Lugano Exhibition of Graphics. He won the Arts Council portrait competition in 1965, the Munster and Leinster Bank competition in 1966, and first prize in the Irish Exhibition of Living Art competition in 1967. In 1985 he was named *Sunday Independent* Artist of the Year, and received the O'Malley Award from the Irish-American Cultural Institute in 1993. His work has been exhibited across Europe and the USA, and in 1991 he was artist-in-residence at the Gate Theatre's Beckett Festival in Dublin, with accompanying works appearing at the Douglas Hyde Gallery.

Adam Buck (1759–1833) was an Irish neo-classical portraitist and miniature painter (his brother Frederick was also an important Irish artist), who worked mostly in London. As well as exhibiting more than 170 miniatures and small full-length portraits at the Royal Academy between 1795 and 1833, he also worked as a painting teacher.

Frederic William Burton (1816–1900) was born in Corofin, Co. Clare. In 1842 he began to exhibit at the Royal Academy, and a visit to Germany and Bavaria that year was the first of many European travels. His best-known paintings, 'The Aran Fisherman's Drowned Child' (1841) and 'The Meeting on the Turret Stairs' (1864), are exhibited at the National Gallery of Ireland.

Mildred Anne Butler (1858–1941), born in Thomastown, Co. Kilkenny, travelled to Brussels and Paris in the early 1880s, studying alongside Walter Osborne and John Lavery. Her works were exhibited in the USA and Japan, and the Kilkenny Museum of Art was renamed The Butler Gallery in her honour.

Michael Canning (1971–) was born in Limerick, where he still lives and works. He graduated from the National College of Art and Design before completing a Fine Art Painting Masters degree in 1999. He has exhibited extensively throughout Ireland and internationally. Recent exhibitions include the Vangard Gallery in Cork, the Hallward Gallery in Dublin, and Galway Arts Centre.

Carey Clarke (1936–) was born in Donegal and educated at St Andrew's College, Dublin, and the National College of Art, where he took up a teaching post in 1963. While at NCA, he was awarded the Royal Dublin Society's prize for portraiture and the Taylor Art Scholarship. He studied painting at the Salzburg Academy in the summer of 1969, and in 1976 took a year's sabbatical to research tempera painting in Florence. In 1985 he received the inaugural Keating/McLoughlin Bursary for Art and a silver medal at the RHA annual exhibition. He began exhibiting in 1956 at the Irish Exhibition of Living Art, and had his first solo show at the Molesworth Gallery in 1966. He was elected a member of the RHA in 1980 and served as Academy President from 1992 to 1995. He is also a member of the Watercolour Society of Ireland.

Harry Clarke (1889–1931), the son of a Dublin stained-glass supplier, benefited from the rebirth of stained glass as an art form at Sarah Purser's An Túr Gloine studios. During his short life he created over 160 stained-glass windows for religious and commercial commissions throughout England and Ireland and further afield. His works include the controversial Geneva Window commissioned by the Irish Free State, illustrating Irish writers and artists.

Diana Copperwhite (1969–) studied Fine Art Painting at Limerick School of Art and Design and The National College of Art and Design, Dublin. She completed a Master of Fine Arts degree at Winchester School of Art, Barcelona, in 2000. Now based in Dublin, she has had recent solo exhibitions with the Temple Bar Galleries, Belltable Arts Centre in Limerick, the Rubicon Gallery, Kevin Kavanagh Gallery, and Limerick City Gallery of Art. Her work is broadly concerned with memory, often incorporating images taken from news media and using layers of paint to semi-obliterate the subject.

Gary Coyle (1965–) was born in Dublin, where he now lives and works, after living in New York and London for nearly a decade. He graduated from the National College of Art in Dublin in 1989 and from the Royal College of Art in London in 1996, where he studied sculpture. He was elected a member of the RHA in 2007 and Aosdána in 2009. His work embraces drawing, photography and, more recently, the spoken word and performance. He had a major solo exhibition, 'At Sea', at the RHA in 2010, and a solo drawing show, 'Hello Darkness', at the Kevin Kavanagh Gallery in 2012.

William Crozier (1930–2011) was born in Glasgow to Irish parents and educated at the Glasgow School of Art. After graduating he spent time in Paris and Dublin before settling in London. Profoundly affected by post-war existential philosophy, Crozier allied himself and his work with contemporary European art, and spent 1963 in southern Spain with the Irish poet Anthony Cronin, which proved pivotal to his development as an artist. On his return to the UK he began a series of skeletal paintings influenced by visits to Auschwitz and Belsen. When he stopped teaching in the 1980s, Crozier's painting blossomed with a new freedom and confidence, his abstract landscapes and still lifes using sumptuous colour to convey emotional intensity. He was elected to Aosdána in 1992 and was an honorary member of the RHA. Crozier's vision is among the most distinguished of recent treatments of the Irish landscape.

Jack Donovan (1934–) was born in Limerick, where he still lives and works. In 1951 he began his studies at the Limerick School of Art, and between 1962 and 1978 was the head of the school, where he taught other artists including John Shinnors, Brian MacMahon and Henry Morgan. In the 1960s he began incorporating collage into his paintings, pasting sections of faces and bodies from magazines and photographs, further distorting the line between the real and the imagined. His individual style comprises elements of humour, politics, history, religion and the human form. In 2004 the Limerick City Art Gallery held a major retrospective of his work.

Jessie Douglas (fl.1893–1928) was a gifted watercolourist, in a similar vein to Rose Barton and Mildred Anne Butler. Little is known, however, about her background, other than that she lived at 1 Windsor Park Terrace in Belfast and was a regular exhibitor with the Watercolour Society of Ireland from 1892 to 1922. The titles of her exhibited works reveal she painted regularly in France, Belgium and the Netherlands, as well as Donegal and Connemara. Her works were exhibited by the Royal Institute of Painters in Watercolour, the Society of Women Artists, the Belfast Art Society (of which she was an honorary member), the RHA and the Royal Scottish Academy among others.

Margaret Egan (c.1950–) was born in New Ross, Co. Wexford. Although she qualified as a draftswoman, she continued her education at the National College of Art in Dublin and studied under the Breton sculptor, Yann Renard Goulet. She now lives and works in Dublin, where she regularly exhibits work in both oils and watercolours.

Robert Fagan (c.1745–1816) was a painter, diplomat and archaeologist. Born in London, the son of Cork immigrants, he spent most of his career in Rome and Sicily. Like other artists in Rome he became involved in dealing in antiquities, and carried out several archaeological digs. As an artist, he made a career from painting portraits, often for travelling British families.

Andrew Folan (1956–), a conceptual artist working in print, photography and sculpture, graduated from the Slade School of Fine Art in 1981. He combines digital processes and print in multi-layered composite photo-montages, and is an active collaborator in scientific, medical and architectural projects. In 2006 he completed a sculptural installation, The Fleet Morph, at the Mater Hospital in Dublin, and in 2008 Anatomy of an Instrument was installed at the Royal Victoria Hospital, Belfast.

Hugh Douglas Hamilton (c.1734–1808) was born in Dublin. He studied art under Robert West at the Dublin Society Schools, concentrating on crayon and pastels in his early career. He lived in London in the early 1760s, where he was often overwhelmed with orders, including his portraits of the British royal family such as Queen Charlotte (1746). Following the advice of fellow artist John Flaxman, Hamilton turned to oil paintings, later painting the portraits of many of Ireland's prominent historical figures of the period including his portrait of Dean Kirwan, which is displayed at the Royal Dublin Society.

Charles Harper (1943–) was born on Valentia Island, and studied at the National College of Art and Design, Limerick School of Art and Graphic Studio Dublin. He also studied film making in Germany. His paintings are well known for their metaphoric themes, including boats, the human form, landscape and angels, usually in painterly expressive form. He has received many national awards for his painting, and exhibits regularly in Ireland and abroad.

Sarah Cecilia Harrison (1863–1941) was born to an affluent family in Holywood, Co. Down. She studied under Alphonse Legros at the Slade School of Fine Art from 1878 to 1885, and travelled widely on the continent as part of her studies. In 1889 she moved to Dublin and established herself as one of Ireland's foremost portrait artists.

Patrick Hennessy (1915–1980), still-life artist, landscape and trompe l'oeil painter, was born in Co. Cork, and won a scholarship to Dundee College of Art where he was taught drawing and fine art painting by James McIntosh Patrick and met the artist H. Robertson Craig. Hennessy was a gifted student, and was awarded a further scholarship which allowed him to study in Paris and Rome. On his return he continued his studies at the Hospitalfield Advanced Art College in Arbroath. In 1939, he exhibited a self-portrait and a still-life at the Royal Scottish Academy, whereupon he returned to Ireland and began life as a professional painter, dividing his time between Cork and Dublin.

Grace Henry (1868–1953), the second of ten children of a Church of Scotland minister, studied drawing and painting in Paris where she met her husband-to-be, Paul Henry. In 1910 a holiday on Achill Island, off the Mayo coast, prompted a move to the west of Ireland in 1912. Grace eventually separated from Henry, who omitted all reference to her in his two-volume autobiography. In her later years Grace Henry travelled extensively; it is largely due to her nomadic lifestyle that many of her paintings have not survived.

Nathaniel Hone (1718–1784) was an Irish-born portrait and miniature painter, and one of the founder members of the Royal Academy in 1768. The son of a Dublin-based Dutch merchant, Hone moved to England as a young man and, after marrying in 1742, eventually settled in London, by which time he had acquired a reputation as a portrait painter. While his paintings were popular, his reputation was particularly enhanced by his skill at producing miniatures and enamels. His sitters included magistrate Sir John Fielding and Methodist preacher John Wesley.

Robert Hunter (c.1720–1803), the principal portrait painter of his time in Ireland, was a native of Ulster, but little is known of his family and early years. He studied art under Thomas Pope. A portrait by Hunter of Tom Echlin, the noted Dublin wit, was engraved and published by Edward Lyons of Essex Street in 1752, and in 1753 Hunter painted a portrait of Sir Charles Burton, Dublin's Lord Mayor; ten years later the Dublin Society awarded him a premium of ten guineas for a full-length portrait of Lord Taaffe.

Mainie Jellett (1897–1944) was born in Dublin, and her early training was at the Metropolitan School in Dublin and with Walter Sickert at the Westminster School of Art. Sickert had trained in Paris and worked with Degas and the French Impressionists, and Jellett's early manner echoed her tutor's particular style of impressionism. Jellett met the artist Evie Hone when studying at Westminster, and the two artists remained lifelong friends. In 1923 she exhibited two cubist canvases at a Dublin Painters' exhibition but was met with hostile criticism. However she persisted, exhibiting in Paris and at the Dublin Radical Club; in 1928 Jellett's work was represented in the Irish section of the exhibition of art at the Amsterdam Olympic Games. The stylised, calligraphic treatment of landscape in Chinese art appealed to Jellett, who saw it as a means of escaping what she believed to be the inherent materialism of naturalistic painting; by 1937 she had fully absorbed the lessons learnt at the Chinese exhibition and incorporated them into her work.

Eithne Jordan (1954–), an Irish visual artist, has had several gallery and museum exhibitions, including at the Gallery of Photography and at the RHA Galleries. She was a Founder member of the Visual Arts Centre, Dublin in 1983. From her emotionally charged expressionistic paintings of the early 1980s, she has turned to urban spaces: car parks, housing estates, factory roofs, underpasses and subway tunnels are all depicted with only a hint of human presence.

George William Joy (1844–1925) was born in Dublin and was initially destined for the military, but following a foot injury was declared unfit for military service. He studied at London's South Kensington School of Art and later at the Royal Academy under John Everett Millais, Frederic Leighton and George Frederic Watts. In 1868 he went to Paris where for two years he was a student of Charles-François Jalabert and Léon Bonnat. Returning to London, he established himself as a history and genre painter, and became a frequent exhibitor at the Royal Academy.

John Lavery (1856–1941), born in Belfast, attended the Haldane Academy in Glasgow and the Académie Julian in Paris. In 1888 he was commissioned to paint the state visit of Queen Victoria to the Glasgow International Exhibition, which launched his career as a society painter. In 1909 Lavery married Hazel Martyn, an Irish-American known for her beauty and poise, who figures in more than four hundred of her husband's paintings. Hazel modelled for her husband's allegorical figure of Ireland, reproduced on Irish banknotes from 1928 to 1975. Lavery was appointed an official war artist in 1914, but ill health prevented him from travelling to France; he remained in Britain and painted the war effort on the home front. After the war Lavery and his wife became interested in their Irish heritage, offering the use of their London home to the Irish negotiators during the Treaty negotiations.

Mary Lohan (1954–) was born in Dublin and studied at the National College of Art and Design; she still lives and works in the city. Over the last ten years or so, she has developed a distinct idiom of expression, and is identified as a leading exponent of Irish landscape painting.

Daniel Maclise (1806–1870) was born in Cork. He was one of the first students to attend the Cork School of Art with fellow students John Hogan and Samuel Forde. In 1827 he moved to London where he attended The Royal Academy Schools. During his early years he supported himself by making pencil portraits, and in 1830 he began his famous series of character portraits for *Frazer's Magazine*. Between 1858 and 1864 he painted a series of large-scale frescoes for the new Houses of Parliament in London. Maclise was attracted to literary and historical subjects; his large painting of 'The Wedding Feast of Strongbow and Aoife' is on view in the National Gallery of Ireland.

Maeve McCarthy (1964–) grew up and studied in Dublin. She is considered one of Ireland's finest figurative painters, working within the traditional genres of landscape, still life and portaiture, using a variety of subjects and experimenting with composition, colour, light and technique. She has received numerous awards at the RHA, and been selected three times for the BP Portrait Award Exhibition at the National Portrait Gallery in London.

Norah McGuinness (1901–1980) was born in Co. Derry, and after living in France, London and New York returned to settle in Dublin in 1940. McGuinness executed vivid, highly coloured paintings in a spontaneous style influenced by Fauvism and Cubism. In addition to paintings, she produced a large number of book illustrations, theatre sets and costume designs. In 1957 she became the founding president of the Irish Exhibition of Living Art, which represented a fundamental break with the RHA academic tradition.

Edward McGuire (1932–1986), portrait and still-life artist, was born in Dublin, and studied painting, drawing and the history of art at the Accademia di Belle Arti di Roma in 1953 and at the Slade School of Fine Art in 1954. In the early 1950s he befriended artists and writers such as Patrick Swift, Anthony Cronin and Lucian Freud. He travelled in France and Italy from 1951 to 1953, and lived on the Aran Islands off Co. Galway from 1955 to 1956. He produced a distinguished body of portraits of Irish cultural figures.

Stephen McKenna (1939–) was born and grew up in London, but while he has lived and worked in various countries since the 1960s, since 1998 he has been based in Ireland. His work achieved international prominence during the 1980s as part of the neo-classical strain of painterly postmodernism. During the 1980s overt pictorial references to classical antiquity gave way to a sophisticated exploration of the enduring value of the time-honoured genres of the still life, interiors, landscapes and seascapes.

Sean McSweeney (1935–), who lives and works in Sligo, is one of Ireland's most highly regarded and original landscape painters. His work is almost entirely based on the small area of shoreline and bogland that surrounds his home on a small peninsula. The repeated use of the rectangular fields relates to the bog holes cut over hundreds of years and which, in winter, fill with brackish water, out of which a rich variety of plants grow in the spring.

Colin Middleton (1910–1983) was born in Belfast and trained at Belfast College of Art. He regarded himself as the only surrealist working in Ireland in the 1930s. His work first appeared at the RHA in 1938 and was followed by his first solo exhibition at the Grafton Gallery in 1944. A damask-designer like his father, he now devoted himself to full-time painting. In 1953 he moved to Bangor, where he designed for the New Theatre. In 1954 he started his career as an art teacher at the Belfast College of Art and at Coleraine Technical School, eventually becoming Head of Art at Friends' School, Lisburn.

Nick Miller (1962–) was born in London and graduated in Development Studies at the University of East Anglia. In that year he moved to Ireland, where he lives and works in Co. Sligo. He has gained critical recognition for his strong contemporary figurative portraits and for his 'Truckscapes', landscapes he paints in the north-west of Ireland from his mobile studio, a converted truck.

William Mulready (1786–1863), born in Ennis, Co. Clare, is best known for his romanticising depictions of rural scenes. In 1792 his family moved to London, where he was educated and was taught painting well enough to be accepted to the Royal Academy School at the age of fourteen. Many of his early pictures are landscapes, but from 1808

he started to build a reputation as a genre painter, painting mostly everyday scenes from rural life. In 1802 he married Elizabeth Varley, a landscape painter.

Liam Ó Broin (1944–) has worked in several media over the last thirty-five years. He studied printmaking at Graphic Studio Dublin under John Kelly, and eventually began teaching lithography there. He studied tapestry weaving under Evelyn Lindsay at the National College of Art and Design and worked with Patrick Pye on two woven pieces. He took up painting in the late 1970s, exhibiting regularly at the Oireachtas and independent artist's exhibitions. In 1980, with the director of Graphic Studio Dublin, John Kelly, he became founder director of Black Church Printmaking Studio.

Roderic O'Conor (1860–1940) was born in Milltown, Co. Roscommon, and studied at Ampleforth College, then at Dublin and Antwerp, before moving to Paris where he was deeply influenced by the Impressionists. In 1892 he went to Pont-Aven in Brittany where he worked closely with a group of artists around the Post-Impressionist Paul Gauguin, whom he befriended. His method of painting with textured strokes of contrasting colours also owed much to van Gogh.

Tony O'Malley (1913–2003) was born in Callan, Co. Kilkenny. He was a self-taught artist, having started painting while recovering from tuberculosis in the 1940s. He resumed his banking career in the 1950s but retired in 1959. In 1960 he went to live in St

Ives in Cornwall and stayed for thirty years, later visiting Ireland during the summers. His early work is figurative, but his interest in expressing inner worlds and the influence of St Ives later led him towards abstraction.

Frank O'Meara (1853–1888) was born in Carlow, the son of a doctor. In 1875 he visited the artists' colonies in Barbizon and Grez-sur-Loing, where John Lavery and Carl Larsson were among his peers. He settled there and eventually befriended Robert Louis Stevenson. In the spring of 1888 he returned to Carlow, where he died either from malaria fever or tuberculosis. Though his output was small, it is easily recognised by its melancholy, autumnal mood and use of subdued but harmonious tones. Five of his works hang at Dublin City Gallery, the Hugh Lane.

Geraldine O'Neill (1971–) was born and grew up in Dublin, where she still lives and works. She studied at the National College of Art and Design, where she completed her BFA in fine art in 1993 and in 2008 completed her MFA. She has lectured in the fine art department of the Dublin Institute of Technology and in the visual art department in St Patrick's teacher training college, Drumcondra. She has exhibited extensively in Ireland.

William Orpen (1878–1931), born in Stillorgan, Co. Dublin, was a fine draughtsman and popular portrait painter in the period leading up to the First World War. Although his studio was in London, he was much involved in the Celtic revival in his native Ireland, and spent time in Ireland painting, befriending Hugh Lane. Like Lavery, Orpen was an official war painter of the First World War, where on the Western Front he produced harrowing drawings and paintings of dead soldiers and German prisoners of war.

Jack Pakenham (1938–) was born in Dublin. His mother died when he was three weeks old, and Pakenham's northern Protestant father moved his children to Northern Ireland. Pakenham graduated from Queen's University, and lived in Ibiza and Dorset before returning to Belfast, where he taught English at Ashfield Boys' High School. In 1990 he retired to devote himself to full-time painting. Recurrent motifs in paintings like the Belfast Series (1989–95) include gagged or blindfolded figures, masked figures who suggest gunmen or hangmen, and limbless or decapitated shop mannequins.

Sarah Purser (1848–1943) was born in Dún Laoghaire, one of eleven children. When her father's grain and milling business failed and he emigrated to America, she moved to Dublin with her mother. After studying in Paris, she returned to Dublin in the 1880s and set about earning a living from painting portraits. Her talent, as well as her sociability and her friendship with the influential Gore-Booths, meant she obtained a large number of portrait commissions. Her other portrait subjects included W.B. Yeats and his brother Jack. A sparkling hostess, she became very wealthy through astute investments, especially in Guinness. Throughout her long life she was active in the Irish art world, being instrumental in the establishment of Dublin City Gallery, the Hugh Lane, the important stained glass studio, An Tur Gloine, as well as the Friends of the National Collections.

Nano Reid (1905–1981) trained at the Metropolitan School of Art in Dublin, where she studied under Sean Keating and Harry Clarke. She then travelled to Paris, enrolling at the Grand Chaumiere. Following her studies in Paris, Reid attended the Central School in London, studying under Bernard Meninsky. Her first solo exhibition was held at the Dublin Painters Gallery in 1934. After returning to Ireland, Reid spent the rest of her life in Drogheda, concentrating on painting aspects of local life and landscapes. In 1950, along with Norah McGuinness, Reid represented Ireland at the Venice Biennale.

Sheila Rennick (1983–) was born in Co. Galway and educated at the National College of Art and Design (NCAD) in Dublin and at Byam Shaw School of Art at Central St Martin's in London, where she took an MA in Fine Art Painting and Art History. Rennick received the CAP Foundation Award in 2004/5 and a painting prize at the Jerwood Contemporary Painters in 2007.

Anne Marjorie Robinson (1858–1924), a miniaturist and sculptor, was born in Belfast. She studied modelling in London in 1911 and was elected member of the Royal Society of Miniature Painters in 1912. Robinson exhibited her paintings on eight occasions at the Royal Academy of Arts between 1911 and 1923.

Sean Scully (1945–) is an Irish-born American painter and printmaker who has twice been nominated for the Turner Prize. He studied at Croydon College of Art and Newcastle University. In the early 1970s he was a recipient of a graduate fellowship at Harvard, and subsequently settled in New York. He has exhibited widely in Europe and the United States.

Una Sealy (1959–) is a graduate of Dún Laoghaire College of Art and Design, and is an Associate of the RHA. She has been involved in many aspects of the arts while maintaining her primary commitment to painting. In 1982 she co-founded Studio 16, one of the first and longest-running group artists' studios in Temple Bar, Dublin. During the 1980s she was very involved in the community arts movement, and was manager of the City Arts Centre in Dublin from 1985 to 1991.

Dermot Seymour (1956–) is a Northern Irish artist. He has been described as a social realist, exploring the anxiety, bewilderment and absurdity of the situation in Northern Ireland and representing it with definite imagery but in an oblique and obscure way. His social realist approach towards Northern Irish politics frequently involves a juxtaposition of images within the Irish landscape, particularly livestock and religious and military symbols. He lives and works in Co. Mayo.

William Sheehan (1894–1923) was a gifted student of the Crawford School of Art. He went on to study art in Dublin, and was then awarded a travel grant to visit Spain, a visit which offered him an opportunity to see many important art works. However, it was not a success financially as the grant was insufficient; he returned early and died tragically a year later.

Edward Sheil (1834–1866) was born in Coleraine, Co. Derry, and moved to Cork at an early age, where he studied at the Cork School of Art. He exhibited his first painting in 1855 at the RHA, and two years later was appointed deputy headmaster of the drawing school. In 1859 Sheil became headmaster, replacing David Wilkie Rainbach, the godson and pupil of David Wilkie. The influence of Wilkie is evident in Sheil's work, in that his paintings are intended to tell a story of both human ambition and human frailty. There is a simple, touching sentimentality in his work, and often a moral and intellectual message that goes beyond the scene depicted.

Stella Steyn (1907–1987) was born in Dublin in 1907 to parents who had moved to Ireland from the town of Akmene on the borders of Latvia and Lithuania. She studied at Alexandra College and the Dublin Metropolitan School of Art and, in 1926, in the company of her mother and fellow artist Hilda Roberts, went to Paris to study at the Académie Scandinave and at La Grande Chaumière. She enrolled at the Bauhaus in Germany in 1931. While in Paris she met James Joyce, who later asked her to provide illustrations for *Finnegans Wake*.

Donald Teskey (1956–) was born in Co. Limerick, graduated from Limerick College of Art and Design, and is now based in Dublin. Since his first solo show in 1980 he has had numerous important exhibitions in Ireland and the UK. A fellowship at Ballinglen Arts Foundation in north Co. Mayo first drew him towards the rural landscape. He applies his paint thickly, and the images reflect his response to the formal elements of shape, form and the fall of light. The result is powerful images of instantly recognisable parts of the Irish landscape.

Harriet Hockley Townshend (1877–1941) was born to a military family. She attended the Metropolitan School of Art, Dublin in 1909 during the period that William Orpen was teaching there, and her work displays his influence. She exhibited at the RHA from 1903 to 1935 and specialised in watercolours and pastels. She was an accomplished portrait artist.

Patrick Tuohy (1894–1930) was born in Dublin, with a severely deformed left hand. His artistic talent was spotted by Pádraig Pearse, who encouraged his father to enrol him in the Metropolitan School of Art. He was taught by William Orpen and became a professor of painting and a member of the RHA. He became associated with the Republican movement, and was selected by James Joyce to paint his father and other family members. Tuohy suffered from manic depression, yet his artwork exhibits a calm and consistent realism. He moved to Columbia, South Carolina, in 1927, thereafter settling in New York, where he committed suicide by gassing.

Charles Tyrrell (1950–) was born in Trim, Co. Meath. He studied painting at the National College of Art and Design, Dublin, graduating in 1974. His first solo show at Project Arts Centre, Dublin, was in 1974 when he was still a student. He lives and works in Allihies on the Beara Peninsula in Co. Cork. He is a member of Aosdána, an affiliation of creative artists, established by the Arts Council of Ireland to honour those artists whose work has made an outstanding contribution to the arts in Ireland. His reputation rests on his later expressionistic work, rich in poetic and cultural allusions.

Sarah Walker (*c*.1960–) is a painter living and working on the Beara Peninsula, West Cork. Born in Dublin, where she studied Fine Art at the National College of Art and Design, she moved to live permanently in Beara in 1991. Much of her work is based on the environment in which she lives and, as well as reflecting the West Cork landscape, is the result of travels to other remote areas of the world including India and Central America.

Jack Butler Yeats (1871–1957) was the youngest son of Irish portraitist John Butler Yeats, and brother of the poet W.B. Yeats. His early artworks were romantic depictions of landscapes and figures from the west of Ireland, and he was also a prolific illustrator, producing images for the Dun Emer and Cuala Industries in Dublin as well as work for London-based publishers. After 1920, sympathetic to but not active in the Irish Republican movement, he began to produce more realistic paintings of life in Ireland.

The New Moon, Moonrise (1908)
John Lavery (1856–1941)

INDEX OF FIRST LINES

Anemones (c.1910)
Roderic O'Conor (1860–1940)

The Window Seat (1901)
William Orpen (1878–1931)

ACKNOWLEDGEMENTS FOR POEMS

Kit Fryatt for her translation of Seán Ó Neachtain's 'Proposal to Úna Ní Bhroin'.

Patrick Crotty for his translation of Úna Ní Bhroin's 'Reply to Seán Ó Neachtain's Proposal'.

'She Being 78, He Being 84' by Seán Ó Tuama from *Death in the Land of Youth*, Cork University Press. © Seán Ó Tuama. Printed with the kind permission of Cork University Press, Youngline Industrial Estate, Pouladuff, Togher, Cork.

Thomas Kinsella for 'Tete a Tete' and translation of 'I Will Not Die For You'.

Gallery Press, Loughcrew, Oldcastle, County Meath, Ireland and the authors for: 'The Globe in Carolina' and 'Two Songs for Doreen' by Derek Mahon, from *New Collected Poems* (2011); 'Nude' by Nuala Ní Dhomhnaill, from *Pharoah's Daughter* (1990); 'Tracks' and 'Crossing' by John Montague, from *New Collected Poems* (2012); 'Be Still as You are Beautiful' by Patrick MacDonogh, from *Poems* (2001); 'The Glasshouse' by Vona Groarke, from *Other People's Houses* (1999); 'On Not Being Your Lover' by Medbh McGuckian, from *Selected Poems* (1997); 'The Smell of Cake' by Seán Dunne, from *Collected* (2005), by kind permission of the Estate of Seán Dunne.

The poems by Patrick Kavanagh, 'Bluebells for Love' and 'On Raglan Road' are reprinted from *Collected Poems*, edited by Antoinette Quinn (Allen Lane, 2004), by kind permission of the Trustees of the Estate of the late Katherine B. Kavanagh, through the Jonathan Williams Literary Agency.

Paul Durcan for 'My Beloved Compares Herself to a Pint of Stout', from *Life Is A Dream*, Harvill Secker, 2009.

'Meeting Point' by Louise MacNeice, from *Collected Poems*, Faber and Faber.

Bloodaxe Books for 'Yearn On' by Katie Donovan.

Dr Sandra Buchanan for 'Song for Straphangers' by George Buchanan.

Douglas Serly for 'Betty O'Brien' translated by Douglas Hyde.

Permission of A P Watt at United Agents on behalf of Nick Laird for 'Lust' from 'The Layered'.

'Lament of Art O'Leary', 'Ordeal by Cohabitation', 'Advice to Lovers', 'The Midnight Court', 'On the Death of his Wife' and 'I am Stretched on your Grave' translated by Frank O'Connor reprinted by permission of Peters Fraser & Dunlop (www.petersfraserdunlop.com) on behalf of the estate of Frank O'Connor.

Peters Fraser & Dunlop for 'The Brewer's man by L.A.G. Strong.

Dedalus Press for 'Na hEallai' by Macdara Woods.

Wisteria
Mildred Anne Butler (1858–1941)

ACKNOWLEDGEMENTS FOR PAINTINGS

The publishers are grateful to the following for their assistance in providing images and information:

Adam's Fine Art Auctioneers & Valuers, 26 St. Stephen's Green, Dublin 2, Ireland   www.adams.ie

Crawford Art Gallery, Emmet Place, Cork www.crawfordartgallery.ie

Graphic Studio Dublin, Distillery House, Distillery Court, 537 North Circular Road, Dublin 1, Ireland www.graphicstudiodublin.com

Solomon Gallery, Powerscourt Centre, 23 S. William St., Dublin 2, Ireland   solomon.gallery@indigo.ie

Royal Hibernian Academy, Gallagher Gallery, 15 Ely Place, Dublin 2, Ireland   www.rhagallery.ie

Limerick City Gallery of Art, Carnegie Building, Pery Square, Limerick   http://gallery.limerick.ie

Dr Michael Purser for paintings by Mainie Jellett (pages 127, 147) and Sarah Purser (pages 94, 169).

Collection: Dublin City Gallery, The Hugh Lane, Charlemont House, Parnell Square North, Dublin 1, Ireland (www.hughlane.ie) for Sarah Cecilia Harrison, 'Mr and Mrs Thomas Haslam' (page 33), Sean Scully, 'John Anthony' (page 100), Frank O'Meara, 'The Widow' (page 159), Frederic William Burton, 'Cassandra Fedele' (page 107).

Hillsboro Fine Art, 49 Parnell Square West, Dublin 1, Ireland (www.hillsborofineart.com) for Sheila Rennick, 'Debs' (page 99).

Rubicon Gallery, 10 St Stephen's Green, Dublin 2, Ireland (www.rubicongallery.ie) for Nick Miller, 'Derval Standing I' (page 87) and Eithne Jordan, 'Split Face' (page 91).

Kevin Kavanagh Gallery, Chancery Lane, Dublin 8, Ireland (www.kevinkavanaghgallery.ie) for Gary Coyle, 'Drawing of a Man' (page 69), Diana Copperwhite, 'Ocular Innocence' (page 85), Dermot Seymour, 'Fish Eyed' (page 134).

Kerlin Gallery, Anne's Lane, South Anne Street Dublin 2, Ireland (www.kerlin.ie) for Stephen McKenna, 'Man Watching the Moon' (page 115).

Waterhouse & Dodd/Fine Art Brokers, 47 Albermarle Street, London for Michael Canning, 'Longlanguish' (page 19).

Jane O'Malley for permission to use 'Callan Landscape, 3 Aspects' by Tony O'Malley (page 57).

Greyfriars Municipal Art Gallery, Greyfriars Street, Waterford for Jack B. Yeats, 'While Grass Grows' © Waterford Municipal Art Collection (page 167).

Pyms Gallery, 24 Farm Street, Mayfair, London, for image of 'Wicklow Labourer' by Patrick Tuohy, private collection (page 112).

DACS for 'While Grass Grows' by Jack B. Yeats © Estate of Jack B. Yeats. All rights reserved, DACS 2013.

IVARO for 'A Cry from the Mountain' (1965) (page 38) © Sean McSweeney; Colin Middleton, 'Esmerelda' (1942) (page 161), 'Bon Voyage' (1976) (page 55), 'Jou Jou' (1939) (page 77) © The Estate of Colin Middleton. All Rights Reserved, IVARO 2014.

The publishers are grateful to the following artists or their estates for their assistance and permission to use their work:

Dermot Seymour for 'Fish Eyed' (page 134).

Liam O'Broin for 'The Kiss, Inferno Canto V' (page 41).

Margaret Egan for 'The Unread Vision' (page 65).

Una Sealy for 'Neighbours' (page 53)

Tom Reid on behalf of Nano Reid for 'The Forest Pool' (page 81).

Charles Harper for 'Landed Angel' (page 141).

Jack Donovan for 'Ballyneety II' (page 47).

Andrew Folan for 'While You Were Out' (page 73).

Sheila Rennick for 'Debs' (page 99).

Stephen McKenna for 'Man Watching the Moon' (page 115).

Brian Bourke for 'Chanteuse' (page 123), 'Self-Portrait in Suburban Garden' (page 153) and 'Don Quixote's Penance No. 2' (page 83).

Nick Miller for 'Derval Standing I' (page 87).

Gary Coyle for 'Drawing of a Man' (page 69).

Diana Copperwhite for 'Ocular Innocence' (page 85).

Donald Teskey for 'The Wind' (page 106).

Pauline Bewick for 'Lovers and Stars' (page 143) and 'Man and Poppies' (pages 75, 76).

Mary Lohan for 'Evening Shoreline, Mayo' (page 155).

Jack Pakenham for 'Your Turn' (page 96) and 'Girl with a Tongue of Water Cried' (page 171).

Michael Canning for 'Longlanguish' (page 19).

Claire Chambers on behalf of the estate of Norah McGuiness for 'River to the Sea' (page 121).

Sarah Walker for 'Bluebell Woods' (page 109).

Eithne Jordan for 'Split Face' (page 91).

The family of Edward McGuire for 'Owl with Falling Oak Leaves' (page 67).

Carey Clarke for 'My Daughter Michelle' (page 79).

Catherine Crozier on behalf of William Crozier for 'The Headland' (page 59).

Lovers in a Landscape
Thomas Bridgford (1812–1878)